THE
INVISIBLE
ASSET

HOW GOOD
COMMUNICATIONS
CAN FIX ALMOST
EVERYTHING

SIMON HEATH

 FriesenPress

One Printers Way
Altona, MB R0G 0B0
Canada

www.friesenpress.com

ISBN
978-1-03-919784-8 (Hardcover)
978-1-03-919783-1 (Paperback)
978-1-03-919785-5 (eBook)

1. BUSINESS & ECONOMICS, BUSINESS COMMUNICATION

Distributed to the trade by The Ingram Book Company

THE INVISIBLE ASSET

HOW GOOD COMMUNICATIONS CAN FIX ALMOST EVERYTHING

TABLE OF CONTENTS

INTRODUCTION

Any organization's most significant asset is largely invisible: it doesn't show up on the balance sheet and there are no KPIs to measure it. And yet it affects every single aspect of the organization from top to bottom. Employees do it all day every day. They do it in meetings, in emails, in chat forums, on PowerPoint, in public, and in private. It fills their calendars. How people communicate within an organization affects productivity, engagement, and effectiveness – in short, communication affects everything.

And yet, communication is largely overlooked as an asset. Individuals are rarely provided with appropriate communication training or coaching. Companies will launch massive projects and the last thing they ask is, "How are we going to communicate this?" Directors are promoted to Vice-Presidents without being told that their entire communication world is about to change. Executives have strategic objectives, but no strategic communication plan. Ask a mid-level manager what the company's strategy is, and they likely won't be able to tell you. Teams get into email fights. And the PowerPoint, oh dear God, the PowerPoint! Every level and layer of an organization relies on communication. And therein lies the opportunity.

I've been an executive communication coach since 1996. I started my career as an actor, director and playwright. I didn't want to work in the corporate world, I wanted to be an artist. But alternative, independent theatre is a hard gig. My first corporate coaching job paid me more in two hours than I could make in a week working in the theatre. Then I had kids, and well, there you go. Most of the time, I am brought in to coach an executive who has communication coaching as part of their professional development plan. I also train small groups, usually teams. And while I enjoy the work, I am aware that it is a little like throwing a hotdog down a hallway – it will have very little impact on the big picture. If employees are given communication training and are then thrown back into the exact same environment they were in before, it is unlikely there will be lasting change. Any effective change needs to involve both the individual and the organization as a whole.

The single biggest thing an organization can do to transform itself (half the businesses I work with are undergoing a Business Transformation Initiative of some kind, most of which will fail to varying degrees) is to focus on their communication culture. Think about it. Every company out there is trying to improve productivity, often through heavy investment in automation. But do they tackle the endless update meetings that produce nothing, involve too many people and take an enormous amount of time to prepare for? Companies commit a lot of time, money and energy to employee engagement surveys, but then miss the most obvious point there is: improve your communication culture and you will improve engagement. And the best thing about communication? It's free.

This book is structured around two main ideas: first, a healthy communication culture needs to be a top organizational priority; second, individuals within the organization need to be provided with the tools and training to be good communicators. In the chapters that follow, I have tried to build a comprehensive approach to tapping into the asset of communication. It is a handbook for building a successful communication culture. Most of what I write is painfully obvious. This stuff is common sense. And that's the beauty of it. The principles I lay out are easy to adopt. If this book is successful, it should put me out of a job. Then I can return to my pursuit of being an artist. Now there's a KPI for you!

SECTION ONE

HOW TO BUILD A HEALTHY ORGANIZATIONAL COMMUNICATION CULTURE

Culture is a fuzzy word and a stubborn reality. I hear the word bandied about all the time. I just Googled the word and found a great definition, but if I start off with a dictionary definition of 'culture', it will sound too much like a high school essay, so I will resist the temptation. I will offer mine. Culture is the sum total of the beliefs and behaviours of an organization. So, big, right? I hear companies trying to build a "Culture of Innovation", or a "Culture of Excellence", or a "Culture of Collaboration". Pardon my cynicism, but I roll my eyes whenever I hear one of those terms. Really? A culture of excellence? A culture of mediocrity and inefficiency is more like the lived reality of most employees. But if culture is part and parcel of everything that a company does, then it's pretty important. And probably pretty hard to change.

What I don't see discussed is the communication culture of an organization. Communication is the invisible link between everything a company does. It touches absolutely everything, and most employees spend the majority of their working lives doing it. Employees communicate with each other verbally and in written format. They use e-mail, video platforms, PowerPoint, text, and chat. They do it within teams, with direct reports, peers, senior leadership, boards of directors, partners, customers and investors. They do it with data, they do it with words, they do it visually with charts and graphs and pictures. Some do it well and some do it poorly. People who do it well often get promoted. But by and large, communication as the fiber of an organization's culture, is ignored.

Sure, sometimes someone like myself is hired to coach an executive to give better presentations. Public facing leaders get some media training. There may be some internal templates. Some organizations might even use the Minto pyramid approach (which is pretty good) as a guideline for how to build presentations. But never, ever, have I seen a company tackle their communication culture head on, and I'm worked with well over a hundred organizations. Which means that these companies develop a de facto culture without purposeful guidance. The communication culture grows organically, by accident, or as a side product. Some of the culture is what is taught in universities. Some is based on what the companies do – the financial services, engineering, or medical fields will all have an approach to communication that is informed by the field they work in. Strategic consulting firms will be different from tax and audit firms. Some will be influenced by their leaders or their boards. Some of it is good, some of it is bad. But because it is an accidental by-product, it is largely untapped as an asset.

When communication is addressed, it is usually for one-offs – "We need to prepare this board deck; How are we going to answer the analysts' questions; What's the message we want to get out at the townhall; How am I going to give this difficult feedback to a direct report?" When we approach communication in this way, it is inextricably linked to the content of the communication. It's not tackled as a thing unto itself, Communication with a capital C. Most companies have internal communications departments, but while they may develop a few templates, their role is largely to develop content. Who is overseeing how the company communicates (and by proxy, how its employees are spending their time)? Usually no one.

So, let's look at the potential benefits of actively working to establish a healthy communication culture:

- Fewer meetings = more time = more productivity
- Shorter, more focused communications (meetings, PowerPoint, emails) = more time, better use of time, better outcomes, more engaged employees
- People-focused communications = more engagement, better collaboration and relationship building, less conflict
- Better communication of strategy = better decision-making, execution of strategy and employee engagement
- More intentional inclusive communication approach = more effectively tap into diversity of employee base and better engagement

But because culture is so big, it takes a concerted effort to, if not change, then at least influence it. It's not reasonable to believe individual employees can overcome organizational inertia. Often when I'm teaching small group programs, one of the participants will say, "This is great, but have you worked with senior leadership/my boss/everyone else in the organization that does it the same stupid way we've always done it?" I'm paraphrasing. And while I believe in the importance of the work I do with clients for their own professional development, a part of me knows that they will largely be drawn back into old patterns, because it's easier to just do what everyone else does.

People like good communication. We love great speakers, exciting ideas. We love clarity, precision of thought. No one likes boring meetings, overly long PowerPoint decks. A poor communication culture grinds us down, deadens us. I'm not just pumping my tires when I say that no one has ever said they didn't enjoy the communication program I deliver. It wouldn't be a stretch to say that employees *crave* good communication. But they can't do it on their own. They need help.

What needs to happen is that good communication becomes the norm and the expectation. This is only achievable if the company makes it an explicit top priority. Not surprisingly, this starts with talking about it. Instead of talking about a culture of excellence, talk about how to communicate. Why it's important to communicate. Show them what good communication looks like. Set clear expectations and provide direction. Make good communication part of the DNA of the company. The benefits are there for the reaping. The first section of this book shows how to do this.

CHAPTER ONE

COMMUNICATE YOUR STRATEGY SO THAT EVERYONE UNDERSTANDS IT

A few years ago, I was working with a client who had just taken over a global portfolio for a Fortune 500 company. She was about to present the strategy for the first time to the global Board of Directors and wanted to prepare with me. I said, "Great! What's your strategy?" She pulled out a 30-page PowerPoint presentation and started to walk me through it. After a few minutes, eyes slightly glazed, I put my hand on the presentation, and said, "No, what's your strategy? If you can't tell me in a minute or less, I guarantee you no one in the organization is executing it." A few weeks later I was talking with a colleague who teaches strategy at a university business school. He was working on a paper that talked about how much difficulty companies have implementing strategy and then measuring the implementation. I jokingly exclaimed, "Half the people I coach can't even remember what the strategy is, never mind implement it!" It was one of those moments when you realize the joke you just made isn't funny. The following chapter is a result of that conversation.

Most organizations do an exceedingly poor job of communicating their strategy. This is no small thing. It is very difficult to deliver on a strategy if it isn't properly communicated within the organization. In fact, I would argue that successful implementation of strategy *depends* on exceptional communication.

A poorly communicated strategy can actually do more harm than good, for three reasons:

- If employees can't understand how the strategy relates to their daily lives, it can cause decision-making that runs counter to the strategy
- Poor communication of strategy causes a lack of employee engagement
- The use of buzzwords causes cynicism and a lack of trust in leadership

I'm going to unpack each of these issues.

If employees can't understand how the strategy relates to their daily lives, it can cause decision-making that runs counter to the strategy

The way most companies communicate strategy is at the same time too abstract and too detailed. When strategy *is* communicated within the organization, it is often done so with the use of buzzwords (Customer-centricity) and platitudes (People, Process, Technology – Really?! You have People, Process *and* Technology?! Amazing!). Strategy is then communicated to the organization in large townhalls, usually through the use of PowerPoint. The presentation starts high-level, with pretty images of happy customers. This is followed by a holistic picture of how all the organization's activities will achieve the goal of the happy customer (usually a slide with a circle, showing how various parts of the business fit into the big picture). It then systematically breaks down the strategy into ever-increasing detailed descriptions of objectives, priorities, tactics, all the way down to individual programs and projects. By the end of the presentation, we have moved from the happy customer to a dense slide with multiple colour-coded columns listing individual projects in 8-point font. Unfortunately, it is unlikely anyone in the audience can read the slide, much less absorb any of it. Too abstract, too detailed.

So, let's look at how this plays out. Let's say an organization is moving towards increased automation. Enormous amounts of capital and resources are being directed towards automating core processes, thereby freeing up employees to do higher value work and providing customer-facing employees with the information they need meet customer expectations. But on the ground, the business needs technology solutions to work in the here and now. There's stuff that's not working and the business is asking the technology division for a work-around. A product owner needs to decide whether to devote staff time and resources to providing a quick fix workaround for the business, which is cheap, serves the business and can be done quickly. But doing this pulls resources away from the longer-term automation project and creates complexity and customization in a system they are trying to simplify and automate. If the strategic direction of automation hasn't been clearly communicated down to the senior manager level, they may very well decide on the work around, effectively running directly counter to the strategy.

Poor communication of strategy causes a lack of employee engagement

Nearly every employee engagement strategy I have seen starts with the need for employees to understand organizational goals. But how can they be engaged if they don't understand how what they do on a day-to-day basis fits in with what they heard the company's senior leadership talking about at the townhall? Strategy rarely trickles down below the Director level (and often not even that far). But it's the people doing the work that need to understand the strategy.

A few years ago, I was working with a company that had Customer-Centricity as it's #1 priority. Everywhere you went, it was Customer-Centric This and Customer-Centric That. I was working with a Project Manager who was in charge of migrating databases to the cloud. When reviewing one of her update presentations, I suggested that instead of simply listing key milestones achieved, she could talk about the strategic importance of the project and how they were supporting those objectives. She looked at me and said, "What do you mean?" Honestly, no idea what I was talking about. I asked, "Isn't your entire company strategy Customer-Centricity?" "Yeah." "And isn't the problem that when a customer calls into a contact centre, the customer service representative can't access a proper customer profile, so they can't be Customer-Centric?" "Yeah." "And don't you have to move all of your databases to the cloud in order to get that information to the CSRs so that they can be Customer-Centric? So, essentially, isn't the entire company's strategy dependent on the project you are leading?" Her eyes lit up. She'd never thought about it, and no one had ever made the connection for her.

Even when leaders do try to communicate strategy, it's often poorly done. Awhile ago, an SVP at a large telecommunications firm asked me to audit one of her monthly departmental meetings. Every month she asked someone in the organization to do a presentation on a project with strategic significance. In the meeting I attended, an employee did an informational presentation about the project she was working on, but failed to articulate why the audience in attendance should care. After the meeting, the SVP asked me for my feedback. I started by telling her that the person in front of me spent the duration of the presentation booking a trip to Florida. The presentation was boring and ostensibly had nothing to do with them. That employee would rather have been anywhere else other than sitting there listening to a presentation about a strategic initiative. Preferably Florida. Not only did the communication of the strategic initiative fail in its desired effect, but it also actively *caused the employee to become disengaged.* The SVP had the right idea by inviting the presenter to talk about the project. But no one told the audience why they should care or how it affected them. If you leave it up to the audience to figure out why they should care, they probably won't.

The use of buzzwords causes cynicism and a lack of trust in leadership.

The use of buzzwords in the communication of strategy is rampant. In some ways, this is understandable, because it can be extremely difficult to communicate high-level ideas that relate to the complexity of running a large business. The higher up the ideas go, the more abstract the language becomes. Part of the problem this causes is that the more abstract the language, the more open to interpretation it becomes; ask ten different leaders to define Agile Methodology and you will likely get ten different responses. We all understand what collaboration means, but what does it look like in the day-to-day reality of people doing the work?

The bigger issue is that buzzwords breed cynicism. I was recently conducting a workshop as part of a leadership development program, and I referenced cynicism. I talked about how I have often heard employees say that to get budgetary approval for an ask, all they need to do is use the right buzzwords and they will get their money. Several people in the program laughed and agreed that this was exactly the case in their organization. I stopped and pointed out how dumb this comment made their leaders appear. And this was a leadership development program! They were the future dummies! But I understand where this cynicism comes from. Somewhere in the organization, there is a PowerPoint slide titled Pillars for Strategic Growth, with a big triangle over top of several rectangles, underneath which are a whole bunch of buzzwords: People; Culture; Innovation; Collaboration. I politely suggested that next time, rather than simply parroting the buzzwords, they try to make the argument that their budgetary ask actually fits within the company's stated strategy. They were duly chastened, but it's amazing the depth and degree of cynicism I hear from clients – invariably aimed at buzzwords.

An effective communication strategy needs to be an integral part of any strategy implementation plan. The following points break down communication of the strategy into two distinct phases: Executive communication of strategy; Rolling out the strategy within the organization.

- Initial executive communication of strategy
  - » There needs to be a communication plan
  - » Effective communication of the strategy starts with clarity
  - » A good articulation of strategy needs to be persuasive rather than directive
  - » The strategy needs to be communicated in simple, clear language
  - » Executives need to be consistent in how they communicate the strategy
- Rolling out the strategy within the organization
  - » The strategy needs to be broken down at each subsequent level of the organization into increasingly small chunks
  - » The strategy needs to be constantly reinforced to make it a living/breathing thing
  - » Communication needs to go hand in hand with action
  - » Course corrections need to be communicated honestly and promptly

Let's take a deeper look at how to achieve this.

Initial executive communication of strategy

There needs to be a communication plan
Honestly, there's very little point in building a strategy if it's not going to be properly communicated. It's not enough to make a presentation at a townhall, then refer back to the strategy every quarter or so. There needs to be a full, comprehensive plan for how it's going to be communicated, by whom, how it should be communicated and how often. Really, the strategy is a recipe for how the company is going to succeed. That's pretty important. So, if it's that important, time and effort needs to be put into a proper communication plan.

*Effective communication of the
strategy starts with clarity*
Clarity and precision of thought are the foundation of communication. All the senior executives need to be able to communicate the strategy in an elevator speech. I constantly see clients trying to 'boil down' their content. It is very difficult to start with a bunch of content and then try to extract clarity. A much better approach is to start with the one-minute version and build out from there. Adding content is easy. Finding clarity isn't. Every executive in the organization needs to be able to communicate the strategy in a manner that the audience walks away thinking, "Well, that makes sense." They shouldn't have to fight to understand it – it should be simple and clear. And frankly, if an executive can't communicate the strategy with that degree of clarity, one has to question how well they understand it.

*A good articulation of strategy needs to
be persuasive rather than directive*

So often, organizations simply tell their employees *what* the company is doing and leave out *why* they are doing it. Employees need to believe in the strategy if they are going to be excited about it. This is the first step to creating engagement. Understanding the why behind the strategy also helps employees make good decisions. The problem with issuing directives (and then breaking everything down into roles and responsibilities) is that as soon as a situation arises that doesn't offer a black and white solution, employees don't have the underlying understanding to be able to respond appropriately. The world is complex, and the decisions we are presented with usually involve varying shades of grey. Offering the rationale behind the strategy empowers employees to make decisions that further the strategy.

*The strategy needs to be communicated
in simple, clear language*

If the strategy is going to play a role in the day-to-day operations of the company, it needs to be simple and clear. This means removing the buzzwords. It means avoiding anything that ends with -ize (monetize; optimize; operationalize). It means avoiding corporate-speak (leverage global footprint to drive efficiencies; deliver just in time customer-focused solutions). Using everyday language and short sentences will make the strategy easy to understand and digestible. The goal is for everyone in the organization to be able to remember and act on the strategy.

*Executives need to be consistent in how
they communicate the strategy*

Many years ago, I met with a colleague whose specialty was debriefing executives after a strategic planning retreat. He told me that typically, only half the executives actually agreed with the strategy, and of the half that did, only half of them had the same interpretation of the strategy. Not much chance of successful implementation if that's your starting place. The senior executives all need to be actively and consistently communicating the strategy. It doesn't matter if the audience is Finance, HR, Engineering, Sales, Marketing or Operations, they need to be hearing the same thing. How it relates to the individual Lines of Business will vary, as it should, but the communication of the overarching strategy should remain consistent across the organization. This requires getting all the senior executives together prior to roll-out to discuss how they are going to communicate the strategy within their verticals. This won't happen by chance; it needs to be a conscious part of the roll-out and all of the senior executives in the organization need to be on board. There needs to be a communication plan, one that goes well beyond the initial townhall.

Rolling out the strategy within the organization

*The strategy needs to be broken down at
each subsequent level of the organization
into increasingly small chunks*

One of the main challenges in implementation is that the people creating the strategy are typically three or four levels removed the people who are implementing it. It needs to be broken down level by level so that at each level of the organization, employees understand the strategy, what it means to them and how they can advance it.

This isn't simply a matter of cascading the strategy, it involves breaking the high-level strategy down into on-the-ground actions. I was working with a VP in technology in a financial services company whose CEO had begun creating video blogs that provided strategic updates. When the VP received these videos, she would forward them to her direct reports as an FYI. She described being at an offsite with some of the Directors that reported to her and by chance hearing two of them talking about how the video had nothing to do with them. She said she was stunned, as these were two of her best Directors, but immediately recognized her mistake: by simply forwarding the video with an FYI, she had missed the opportunity to break down what was important for them. It would only have taken two or three sentences instead of the FYI. Simply cascading information is a missed opportunity.

Engaging multiple layers within the organization needs to part of the communication plan. Even before the initial roll-out of the strategy, a communication plan needs to involve multiple layers of leadership: SVPs need to work with VPs to ensure they understand the strategy and have a plan for working with their Directors on what it means to them; VPs need to work with their Directors to ensure they understand the strategy and have a plan for working with their direct reports and what it means to them; and so on.

Once the strategy has been rolled out, each of these levels of executives need to follow up the initial roll-out with team meetings that break down the strategy for their teams. A good idea is to pull two or three slides from the initial presentation that the VPs and Directors will use as the basis for discussion at these meetings.

The strategy needs to be constantly reinforced to make it a living/breathing thing

Reinforcing the strategy is more than simple repetition. It involves constantly connecting the dots for direct reports. It involves looking for real life examples, in meetings, on phone calls, in one-on-ones, to help bring the strategy to life so that it can affect day-to-day decisions and actions. At minimum, it means taking those two or three slides from the initial roll-out of the strategy and coming back to them at every monthly meeting.

One of my ongoing clients over the years was a large company that was implementing SAP enterprise software across the business. This was a *huge* undertaking. At the outset of the project, the company was administering HR services for more than 150,000 employees through the use of Excel spreadsheets, which was a big time-consuming mess. The project included everything from HR to Point of Sale to Supply Chain. After the first year, the project was facing massive challenges, and the President of the company hosted a nationwide townhall, announcing that SAP Implementation was now Priority #1. I happened to be teaching a course on the day of the townhall and one of the participants was a Senior Director of Loss Prevention. Essentially, he had a lot of security guards in his organization, and quite correctly figured that they would have watched the video of the town-hall and thought that SAP had nothing to do with them. He decided to put together a presentation for his people arguing that their daily actions had a direct impact on SAP. He argued that SAP is based on quality data and that the enemy of SAP is bad or missing data. He was able to link the townhall back to ensuring the SKUs from recovered items were entered into the system, all the way to opening up the box that has been sitting in the staff room for the past several months and ensuring that any items found were duly recorded. It was a brilliant example of how a mid-level executive needs to take the high-level strategy and make it tangible.

Leaders within the organization need to be *looking for opportunities to reinforce the message.* As obvious as it sounds, you can't capitalize on a leadership opportunity if you don't recognize the opportunity. Leaders need to be looking at all their communication opportunities, from e-mails to phone calls and meetings, as opportunities to bring the strategy to life.

Communication needs to go hand in hand with action

Of course, it's not enough to simply communicate the strategy effectively. Words without action are corrosive and breed distrust. Employees develop an immunity to the words that carries well into the future – in fact builds - and the people that have been there the longest (and as such are very influential) learn to dismiss any new initiative as flavour of the month. Leading by example is essential. But the biggest impact is felt when words and action go hand in hand. For example, celebrating successes has become a standard part of departmental meetings (or, at least, it should). This is a perfect opportunity to not just celebrate the success, but to link it back to the strategic objectives. If someone does something that is directly linked to the strategy, call it out!

Course corrections need to be communicated honestly and promptly

I can't tell you how many companies I have worked with that trumpet their focus on the customer and then promptly close a contact centre. Or talk about developing a culture of innovation and remove funding from R&D. Employees watch senior leaders very closely and if they say one thing and appear to do another, trust in leadership will immediately take a hit. Trust is a very hard thing to develop and can be lost in the blink of an eye. If the organization is changing directions, communicate it to the employees quickly and honestly. Sometimes a decision appears to run counter to the strategy but is actually consistent: maybe data shows that customers have expressed a desire for self-service solutions and by closing call centres the company is able to redeploy finances that can better serve customer needs. Regardless of whether it is a true course correction, or just appears to be, senior leadership needs to be constantly communicating with the employees.

This might sound obvious, but a company's strategy is central to its success. But how can it execute on that strategy if the employees aren't living and breathing it? And how can the employees be living and breathing it if they can't remember what it is? Without good communication, even the best strategy implementation plan is susceptible to failure. Successful implementation of strategy *depends* on exceptional communication. By weaving communication into the fabric of the implementation plan, the plan is much more likely to succeed.

CHAPTER TWO

COMMUNICATE WITH EMPLOYEES LIKE THE SMART HUMAN BEINGS THEY ARE

Honestly, you'd think a lot of organizations believe their employees are idiots. I can't tell you how many times I've seen the same picture of a rock climber hanging off the underside of an outcropping (I hope that poor sucker's getting royalties). Or been told that we're at the Everest base camp, but it will take teamwork to reach the summit. Or that we're like an F1 race car. Or that We Win As One. Tired analogies and corporate buzzwords aren't the way to motivate employees. *Stop using slick marketing to communicate internally!* Your organization's employees are smart. They're human beings. Try talking to them like smart human beings.

Many years ago, I was asked to help a company prepare for an Annual Kick-off. The company was spending an enormous amount of money to bring 1800 store managers together for the first time ever. I was invited to the war room, where internal communications people, HR professionals, business leaders and an assortment of others had been planning the event for several months. My first question, as always, was, "What's the one idea you want the audience to walk away with?" My contact responded immediately, "Oh, we've got that. It's For the Customer!" I could see these words emblazoned on tote bags, memory sticks and lanyards strewn about the room. My response was: "No, it's not. I just saw a presentation about employee fingerprint scanning for payroll. 'It's For the Customer' is your slogan, and really it should be 'It's For the Shareholder!' What I mean is, what is the one real thought you want them to have in their minds when they fly home, hungover, and think back on the past three days? One idea they didn't have before they came." She thought for a minute, then responded, "Well, really we want them to believe that Corporate has its shit together." There you go. That's an idea worth communicating. Maybe change the language a bit.

I chose to place this section on language in the organization part of the book rather than the section on individuals, because the leadership of the organization sets the tone. We talk the way our bosses talk. Language use in the workplace is a bigger problem than most of us acknowledge. A lot of professional communication is excruciatingly boring. I get it, we're being paid to be there, it's hard to make reviewing the dashboard exciting. But we don't have to make it worse through the words we choose. Language has the opportunity to bring an idea to life, or to bury it. The language we use can be the difference between an audience hearing, accepting and retaining our ideas or having them flow in one ear and out the other.

The biggest threat to the effective use of language is abstract jargon and buzzwords. This language is overly inflated, industry-specific and often so abstract that it means different things to different people. The examples of this are endless, from "synergistic relationships" to "next-generation leadership potential" to "strategic alignment". These words are designed to sound important. Most damaging is that they are words that we as people would rarely use outside of the work-place. We don't utilize the lawnmower to optimize the length of the grass. We mow the lawn. When we adopt language that we would never use in our personal lives, we distance ourselves from the ideas we are trying to communicate. As a result, our ability to persuade is reduced. We are at our most persuasive when we are able to show our own conviction. Human to human.

Of course, no one likes corporate language. But we all seem to use it when it's our turn to speak. Why? Generally, the reason given is that it's 'the culture' to use this type of language. We feel that it's expected of us. In other words, we use it because everyone else does. This book is about changing your communication culture and one of the easiest places to start is with the language you use. The people we tend to look up to are the people who convey their ideas with clarity and passion. We can feel the energy of their ideas because they give us access to them through their words. This is the opportunity that language presents us with.

I'm going to describe five basic principles that will help you use language to its full potential:

- **Use clear, concrete language**
- **Use personal, conversational language**
- **Use short sentences**
- **Use positive language**
- **Use language with some life to it**

Use clear, concrete language

When speaking or writing, fight to find exactly the right word to express your thoughts. Abstract language leaves room for interpretation. An example would be the word "sustainable". If a developer, a government official and a community activist all agree to "sustainable development", it's almost guaranteed that they would mean different things when they use this term. Likewise, someone in Finance, Operations or HR would also have a different interpretation of the word 'sustainable'. Unfortunately, we often don't discover this difference of interpretation until after the fact, when it is too late. Clear language helps us avoid these differences of interpretation. By using clear, concrete language, I do not mean dumb down the language. People often refer to the KISS principle (Keep It Simple Stupid) when communicating. Your audiences aren't stupid, and your ideas are challenging; use words that are going to excite your audiences. If you fight for clarity, simplicity is often the by-product. It doesn't necessarily work the other way around.

Use personal, conversational language

Communication happens between human beings. We are trying to connect our thinking with another human being through the use of words. The more you can use personal pronouns, the more your audience will feel a connection to you and what you are saying. So, yes, this means saying, "I", "You" and "We" rather than "it was deemed necessary", "there was an organizational driver" or any other depersonalized way of framing an idea. Once you start using personal pronouns, you will find that you will naturally be drawn to a more conversational way of speaking. It doesn't matter if it's an e-mail, a presentation or an update to Senior Leadership, the more personal and conversational your language, the more effective you will be at getting the audience to receive your ideas.

Use short sentences

Run-on sentences are difficult to follow. I am very blunt with my clients: run-on sentences display sloppy thinking; crisp sentences reflect crisp thinking. The reason for this is that long sentences tend to have a lot of commas, which suggests multiple idea fragments. These types of sentences are hard to follow and hard to remember. If you find yourself losing your train of thought, your sentences are probably too long. Using short sentences takes practice. You can use e-mails and conference calls to practice. The shorter your sentences, the better your audience will listen.

Use Positive Language

When I tell clients to use positive language, I don't mean "Use fluffy, turn-a-frown-upside-down language." I mean structurally positive. I recently finished working with an audit department that was working to become a 'trusted advisor' to the business. Many of the auditors wanted to work on how to overcome unreceptive, defensive audiences. When I listened to one of the auditors give a sample of what they would present to the business, it was filled with, "There's a risk exposure because..., Your internal processes aren't..., There's too much..., You don't have proper controls..." I said they could probably just save time by writing "You don't know what you're doing" on a slide. The exact same findings could be put forward positively – "There's a significant opportunity to improve..." The simple example I often give is a manager speaking to their team. Here are two options:

- "There's no way we're going to meet our targets unless we make significant changes."
- "If we're going to meet our targets, we need to make significant changes."

These are only subtly different. The big difference is that the first, negative statement will lead to a list of all the reasons we won't meet our targets. The second, positive statement, will lead to more forward-looking ways to meet our targets. Positive language doesn't just change how the audience receives the statement; it also changes the structure that follows.

Use language that has some life to it

Keeping your focus at work can be hard, particularly at 2:00 in the afternoon when your blood sugar is low. Don't make it harder on your audience by using abstract, lifeless language. Choose words that excite. Adjectives inject energy into a meeting, as do metaphors or alliteration or parallel structure. Remember all those things you learned about in high school English class? Now's your chance to use them. Rather than endless run-on sentences, use some short sentences to punctuate a point. Listen to what you're saying. Does it sound boring to you? If it does, chances are it does to your audience as well. You don't have to write a haiku but try using language with some life to it.

Effective use of language is essential to good communication. It isn't window-dressing; it is the embodiment of your ideas. Language can offer the audience an access point to your ideas and a reason to be inspired. If they have to fight their way through dense jargon, run-on sentences and impersonal language, there's a good chance many of them will be lost along the way. Be courageous in your choice of words and your audiences will thank you.

CHAPTER THREE

BUILD A COMMUNICATE PLAN FOR EVERY PROJECT

If you're nearing the end of a project and someone asks, "So, how are we going to communicate this?", it's already too late. When I hear clients discuss Lessons Learned on why a project didn't go as planned, I'll often hear them say, "We dropped the ball on the change management piece." If we pass this through the plain-language translator, this often means, "We did a crappy job of communicating it." Word gets out pretty quickly about a project and if you wait until the end, people will already have decided what they think about it. If the rationale behind a project isn't clearly communicated at the beginning, as well as throughout a project, it runs the risk of going off the rails.

One company I worked with was working on a project called One Acme (I've used the Roadrunner company to protect the guilty). They were trying to consolidate their platforms so that their customers for all the various lines of business would have one point of contact in the company. Around halfway through the project, I worked with the project leader on a presentation to the team to stop them from going off to sign individual contracts with different vendors. She was baffled – the name of the Project was One Acme! And yet, the people working on the project were doing the exact opposite of the project's intent. How could they have lost sight of the fact they were trying to unify everything?

Another company was doing an enterprise-wide software implementation. There was conflict between the business and IT throughout the project. At one point, my fiery VP of IT client exclaimed in exasperation, "The business thinks the platform is going to transform their business. But no! They need to transform their own business and we will support them with the implementation!" I said, "That's great. Did you tell them that?" He paused. "No." I asked, "Do you think it would have been helpful if that had been communicated at the beginning of the project and then reiterated throughout?" He said, "Yes. No more fighting." There was a fundamental philosophical difference of opinion that had never been spoken out loud which was the source of much of the conflict (and wasted time and money). It was because when the project kicked off, everyone just put their head down and started working, without taking the time to communicate the big picture first.

Yet another company underwent a massive shift from their traditional reporting structure to a matrix-style reporting structure where employees had solid line reporting to their managers and dotted line reporting into a different group. The goal was to break down silos, improve communication and collaboration. The problem? They didn't communicate the change properly, so people kept doing what they were used to doing. Rather than increase efficiency, it created chaos. It took years to fix.

The common theme in all these examples is a lack of a proper communication plan for the project. And these are big, expensive projects we're talking about – often hundreds of millions of dollars. They have executive sponsors, seasoned leaders, project managers with clear roles and responsibilities. But so often, communication is a blind spot, an afterthought. The success of any project depends on how it is communicated. A good communication plan should have three elements:

- **What is the reason for the project?**
- **Who needs to be communicated with during the project and how?**
- **How will it be communicated to the broader organization?**

What is the reason for the project?

I'm going to sound like a broken record on this (those were those black things with a hole in the middle that used to play music) but communicating the *why* is absolutely essential. Everybody involved in the project needs to know why we're doing it. Everybody affected by the project needs to understand why we're doing it. Any third-party vendors should know why we're doing it. All the executives need to understand why we're doing it. Sometimes even the investors and analysts need to know why we're doing it. They need to be told before the project starts. They need to be told at the kick off meeting. They need to be reminded of it during the project. The why needs to be communicated when the pilot project is rolled out. The why needs to be communicated when training is being provided. Everybody needs to understand why we're doing it. And then, when we do a debrief and discuss lessons learned, we need to start the conversation with why we did the project. It's extremely important that everybody understands why we're doing it. Okay, point made.

Who needs to be communicated with during the project and how?

Any project manager reading this will likely roll their eyes at this question, and go, "Duh." Every project will have all the various groups represented, there will be weekly update calls with lots of people on the call and even more cc'd. Every month there will be a broader update where senior leadership is walked through the dashboard. Standard practice.

And yet, almost every legal team I've ever worked with says they wish they were involved in the project earlier. So often, legal is provided with information, or a deal, at the last minute and are asked to rush approval. And, of course, they slam on the brakes, find problems that could have been easily avoided had they been involved earlier and force rework that adds time and budget to the project. I actually worked with a company where the COO had a lawyer on his staff in operations to negotiate with the company's legal team to try to get projects approved more quickly! I see the same things happen with the risk group not being involved early enough and then slowing the project down. Simply engaging with the legal or risk teams earlier in the process would help avoid a lot of problems.

A comprehensive communication plan needs to look at all the areas of the business that need to be communicated with, when they need to be communicated with and how they need to be communicated with. And, if in doubt, involve them earlier, and communicate more often, than you think is necessary. I once had a client who defined the difference between a project manager and a project leader as follows: "A project manager ticks boxes to make sure the project is on track. A project leader is always looking ahead and proactively communicating with whoever needs to be communicated with." Communication and leadership are inextricably intertwined.

How will it be communicated to the broader organization?

One company I worked with undertook a major project that they dubbed The Speed of Change (remember what I said about not using slogans to communicate internally?) This was a massive, company-wide, top-secret project, so of course everyone knew about it. It covered all parts of the business and involved a restructuring as one component of the project. The real purpose of the project was to modernize the organization so that it could be more competitive. It involved IT upgrades. New specialized teams with new areas of focus. But as word filtered out across the organization, all it became known as was a huge downsizing. By keeping the project a secret, it created the opportunity for all sorts of rumours to run rampant. It created distrust. Engagement went down. Many of the company's employees dusted off their resumes and left the company before they could be downsized. And it missed an opportunity to get the employees excited about the direction of the company. There were a huge number of positive things in the project, including many that employees had been asking for – but because of the lack of a communication plan, these positives were lost.

Communication can't be an afterthought. "How are we going to communicate this?" should be asked before any project kicks off and should be woven into the fabric of the communication plan. Communicate it well, and your chances of a successful project go way up.

CHAPTER FOUR

TACKLE YOUR MEETING CULTURE – FEWER MEETINGS, MORE EFFECTIVE MEETINGS

Meetings have always been a massive part of having a corporate career. And they've always been a bit of a problem. But physical meetings in real buildings had some limitations. They were limited by the size and availability of a room (remember when most meetings started with an argument about who had booked the room?) We had to physically walk from one meeting room to another. Sometimes we had meetings over lunch (they were called Lunch Meetings). Suddenly, when the pandemic hit and we moved to video platforms, there were no longer any limitations, and meetings swept in to fill every available minute of space there was. I was speaking with a client recently who confessed to using a week of personal holidays to pretend he was on vacation, so that he could stay home and get some work done. His rationale was that it was more relaxing than going on vacation.

Most of the discourse around meeting culture focuses on individual responsibility. Managers are encouraged to look for standing meetings that provide no value and cancel them, people are encouraged to ask if a meeting needs to be weekly or if it could be bi-weekly. These are important, and I will address them in the second half of this book, but it's not reasonable that one individual is going to be able to resist the culture of the organization on their own. It is the responsibility of leadership to create the expectation of an effective meeting culture.

One organization I work with has monthly 4-hour business unit meetings. There are 12 business units and approximately 80 people on each call. A large group from each business unit spends the better part of a week preparing for the call. I was on a call with a finance executive from the company and made an offhand comment about wanting to assign a dollar figure to those meetings. He gamely exclaimed, "I can do that!" and started doing the math, pen on paper. It was a rough estimate, true back-of-the-envelope math, but it came out in the $7M-$10M range. For a company struggling to increase productivity, that's a pretty obvious one to me. What if the meeting was 20% shorter (48 minutes), with 20% fewer people on the call (16 people) and 20% less prep time (I don't know)? You can't tell me you can't achieve the same objectives with a 3+ hour meeting, 64 people on the call and less prep time on the deck of slides. And all the savings go directly towards productivity. Now extrapolate out and apply this to all meetings. There are your productivity gains right there.

Of course, communication isn't just about productivity. It's also about engagement, problem-solving, and inclusion. At the beginning of 2023, the tech company Shopify cancelled all meetings of three or more people in one sweeping edict. In doing so, the company estimates it freed up 76,500 hours of employee time, which given the fact they recently laid off 10% of their workforce, is time that is sorely needed for their employees to do actual work. The purge was deemed temporary, and it will be interesting to see how much chaos results, and how much of the old meeting culture creeps back in. Meetings are important. But there are a lot of stupid, pointless meetings. So, the trick is to get rid of the stupid meetings and focus on how to make meetings better. Because meetings are just another form of communication.

Of course, if it was easy, it would already be done. That's why the organization needs to step in. The organization needs to set the culture and set the example. There are a few simple things that can be done:

- **Make senior meetings concise**
- **Provide templates for updates**
- **Set expectations through your internal communications and stick to them**
- **Make meetings inclusive**

Make senior meetings concise

This is all about setting an example. The old "do as I say, not as I do" approach to management (or parenting, for that matter), doesn't work well. Any meetings with senior leadership should have a crisp, clear agenda, should be concise and focused, and should stick to the agenda. Culture starts at the top.

Provide templates for updates

It's not reasonable to expect meetings to be more concise without providing support on how to do that. Updates are the most common form of meeting on the planet. From the day we start working as an intern to the day we retire as CEO, we will be giving and receiving updates. And for some bizarre reason, there is no consistency on how updates are structured. Some direct reports will go through a list of everything they did last week. Others resent they have to report to you and don't want to have to do an update because they'll tell you if there's a problem. IT updates will provide a list of obscure acronyms and launch dates, along with the number of tickets resolved. Sales will have endless columns of numbers, some highlighted in red. Don't even get me started on Finance.

Is all this information dumping useful? Are people even paying attention to the content? Everyone I have ever talked to who receives updates, cares about two things, with a subset.

- Are things on track?
- Where are they headed?
  » Do you need anything?

Can someone explain to me why every single human being on the planet doesn't structure our updates that way?! The following template can be used across the organization:

- What is the one main idea you want audience to walk away with?
- Are things on track?
  » Justify with supporting data
  » Why or why not?
- What's coming next?

> » How will upcoming challenges be addressed?
> » Do you need anything?

There. Boom. Done.

Other, non-update meetings can have a similar template for the agenda:

- What's the main goal of this meeting (if this question can't be answered, cancel meeting)
  - » Why is it important to attendees?
  - » What are we hoping to achieve?
  - » Is there action required?
  - » Who needs to attend?

By providing templates for how to better structure the content of meetings, they will be more productive, tend to be shorter, and be a more valuable use of the participants' time.

Set expectations through your internal communications

Getting rid of meeting bloat won't be easy. Even if you do make gains, it will come creeping back. Standing meetings don't get cancelled even after they no longer serve a purpose. The list of people invited to meetings will continue to grow unless the lists are routinely culled. People need to be constantly encouraged to keep meetings tight and to a minimum. Set targets if you have to. One executive I coached said that when he took over the engineering department of a technology division, they did a time audit and found out the engineers were spending 70% of their time in meetings and 30% of their time doing engineering work. He decided to flip those numbers and actively and aggressively communicated that target. It took commitment and effort, but in less than two years they were able to hit their target of 30% of their time spent in meetings and 70% of their time doing engineering work. That's a whole lotta productivity right there. And happy employees, doing what they were hired and trained to do.

During the pandemic, a lot of companies instituted No Meeting Fridays. Then they worried people were just taking long weekends, so they instituted No Meeting Thursdays. But then some other companies had No Meeting Tuesdays, and it didn't match up with their partners' No Meeting Thursdays, so eventually they kinda gave up and it all disappeared. Likewise, some companies encourage blocking time in the calendar for reflection, realizing that people need time to reply to emails, or think, or do work. But it's left up to the individual to fend off all the requests for their time and eventually that blocked-off time falls by the wayside. If my leader asks for a meeting during my blocked off time, am I going to say no? If a direct report notices I have a blank spot in my calendar and asks if I have time for a quick call, didn't I say I have an open-door policy?

Individuals can't fight the tide on their own. They need the organization to actively communicate what the expectations are around meetings, constantly reinforce those expectations and provide the templates to help people get there.

Make meetings inclusive

One of the biggest problems with meetings is that they often focus exclusively on the subject matter. A while back I was working with a highly analytical finance executive. When we got together (virtually) for one of our regular coaching sessions, he described a pair of his meetings that he approached very differently. "One meeting was on a Friday. It was a check-in for a very large, very frustrating project. The project isn't going that well and people are clearly frustrated. My instinct is to drive a meeting's agenda no matter what. I always want to make sure we stick to the agenda and push through to the end. This meeting didn't go very well, and the end result was that we decided we had to meet again. I thought about this over the weekend and on Monday, I was leading a very similar type of meeting – big project, stuck in the mud, people feeling very dispirited. This time, instead of driving the agenda when things started to bog down, I stopped the meeting and asked everyone how they were feeling. We went around and people described their frustration and lack of motivation. I responded by saying that this made sense. I've been with the company for fifteen years, and the project we are working on has been a problem the entire time – we're just finally having the courage to tackle it, and so of course people are feeling frustrated. We then moved back into the agenda, and it turned into one of the most productive meetings we've ever had. I never would have thought it before but stopping to check in on how people were feeling was the most efficient way of conducting the meeting."

If we are judicious about when to call a meeting and who to invite, it allows us to ensure that meetings are used to include everyone, so that they feel heard, and the group receives the benefit of a multiplicity of perspectives.

Fewer stupid meetings is the starting point. Making meetings better is the ultimate goal. If you use people's time well, they will show up and be engaged.

CHAPTER FIVE

RECOGNIZE THE IMPORTANCE OF YOUR DIRECTOR-LEVEL EMPLOYEES

I've often argued that the two biggest shifts in a person's career are when they move from individual contributor to people leader and when they move from Director to Vice-President. When employees move into manager roles, they are often provided with some kind of training on how to manage people. Unfortunately, the same can't be said for when Directors become Vice-Presidents. And yet, I would argue that the ability of this band of executives to effectively communicate is absolutely critical to organizational success.

Over the course of my career, I would say that by far and away, the biggest segment of my clients have been Directors or Senior Directors. Maybe that's because there are more of them than there are senior executives. Most directors achieve their position because they're smart, work hard, and know their business inside and out. The position of Director is the pinnacle of a certain career trajectory. When Directors are promoted to Vice President, they often learn the hard way that what made them successful up until that point no longer serves them. It's no longer possible to be on top of every detail. Working hard isn't enough, in fact it often leads to becoming a bottleneck, micro-managing, preventing those under you from developing and burn-out. Being a Vice President is much more about strategic thinking, delegating, and not surprisingly, communicating. Unfortunately, nobody tells them this. I was recently talking to a Vice-President about the coaching program I would be providing to the Director he was looking to as his successor, and he responded, "I wish someone had told me this when I became Vice President. It would have saved me ten years of hard lessons."

Directors are the funnel through which all communication happens. I often describe the Director role as the narrow part of an hourglass. All the high-level, abstract, strategic content funnels down to the Director and it is their job to translate the abstract strategy into concrete action for their teams. Strategy often means nothing for the people doing the work and it is the Director's job to make it meaningful and tangible. At the same time, senior executives often have no clue what's actually happening in the day-to-day operations of the company. All they see are reports and dashboards and PowerPoint presentations. It is the Director's job to translate the on-the-ground reality into content that is relevant to the more abstract strategic concerns of the executive. In other words, Directors need to be fluent in two languages, understand both the real-world activities of the company as well as the abstract strategy and be able to successfully translate between the two. But many Directors don't translate, they simply cascade. They will cascade the information from above to their team. They will compile the data from their organization and present it to their leaders. This isn't effective. The key to being a good Director is in being able to understand both worlds and translate between the two. And they are often tasked with flipping the hourglass over multiple times per day as they move from meeting to meeting. Sounds hard, doesn't it?

Many Directors never get beyond being good at what they do. Operational. And that's fine, that's a successful career. But to advance beyond Director, a shift needs to happen. I've had so many clients who say they want to be seen as leaders rather than do-ers. As one Director client put it: "I'm seen as the person who gets shit done."

If you want to build a good communication culture, Directors need to be at the heart of it:

- **Provide communication training to new directors**
- **Involve Directors in strategic planning**
- **Always involve Directors in communication rollouts**

Provide communication training to new directors

Directors spend a shocking amount of time building PowerPoint slides. It is primarily Directors who are building content for their senior leaders to present at executive meetings or even Board of Director meetings. One dirty little secret of the corporate world is how much time executives spend editing their direct reports' work. A Vice President has to present at an executive meeting, and they ask some of their direct reports for a couple slides on whatever topic they are to present on. When they receive the slides, they are usually way too dense, with too much detail, and information that isn't of use to senior executives. The slides also usually arrive at the last minute, and the VP is forced to edit the slide themselves. Editing slides is not a good use of an executive's time. This is an example of how the Director needs to do a better job of translating the on-the-ground reality into useful points for the executive.

A second little dirty secret is that while team meetings are a standard part of professional life, a lot of people don't know what to do with them. The typical approach is that the person running the meeting (in this case the Director), might pass on some information to the team from management and then the team members go around and talk about what they're working on. The thing is, the Director has probably already talked to each team member in their 1:1, and what each team member is working on may or may not have anything to do with the other team members, and if it does, they've probably already talked to them. So, we know we're supposed to have team meetings, but the value is often hard to pinpoint. The team meeting would be much more effective if it was an opportunity to take the strategic objectives of the team and discuss how they're doing implementing them and look for creative ways to do better. This is an example of how the Director could do a better job of taking the abstract strategic objectives and work with the team to make it a reality (all the while promoting teamwork, which is what the meeting is supposed to be about).

New Directors shouldn't be expected to just figure this out on their own. The same way organizations will provide new managers with training, we need to provide new Directors with training. It doesn't even have to be expensive training, it can be an internal, 'So You've Just Been Promoted to Director... Here's What You Need to Know' program. At the centre of the training should be:

- How to effectively communicate up
- How to effectively communicate down

A well-trained, effective Director group is one of the most powerful assets an organization can have. And once again, it's all about communication.

Involve Directors in strategic planning

Some organizations do this, some don't. They should. As the narrow part of the hourglass, Directors have critical knowledge of the organization that needs to be incorporated into strategic planning. So many times, I've heard a Director client talk about a new organizational initiative and say, "That'll never work." First of all, the strategic initiative shouldn't have been planned without the input of the Directors. Secondly, it will be up to the Directors to implement the initiative – if they don't believe in it, it's destined to fail.

By involving Directors in the strategic planning process, you will also be developing their ability to think strategically. Directors are the talent pool from which will come the future leaders of the organization. It's better to teach them to think strategically before they are promoted than on the fly.

Always involve Directors in communication rollouts
In earlier chapters, I've discussed the importance of having a communication plan for rolling out both strategy and all projects. Unfortunately, Directors are rarely included in these plans. For the annual kick-off, the CEO usually talks about strategic priorities, then the heads of business units talk about what it means for their individual businesses, maybe there's a VP or two that chimes in, but that's about as far as it goes. But it's the Directors that are going to have to communicate it with their teams. And if there's pushback, it's the Directors that are going to hear about it, and have to address the concerns, not the senior executives.

I was working with an SVP of Sales for a Telco recently, who was planning a restructuring of the sales team – one that fundamentally altered the salespeople's roles by categorizing them as Hunters (prospecting new clients) or Farmers (organic growth from the existing customer base). He was announcing the change over a call with several thousand people and knew that there would be a lot of anxiety and questions that came with the announcement. But no one's going to say anything on a call with the SVP. He personally was quite passionate that it was going to be good for the salespeople and they would come to love it, but he was worried about their initial response. When I asked him if he planned to meet with the Director team before the call to discuss what the questions and concerns might be and how they could respond to them, his eyes lit up. "That's a great idea!" he said. The thought of involving the directors in the communication roll-out had never entered his mind.

Directors have one of the toughest and most important jobs in any organization. They take a lot of shit, are responsible for everything and control nothing. If we're being really honest, the job of VP is often a lot easier than Director. Organizations that recognize their importance and offer them access and support are doing themselves a huge favour.

CHAPTER SIX

IMPROVE COMMUNICATIONS
BETWEEN BUSINESS UNITS

Regional Operations thinks Corporate is slow and bureau-cratic with no understanding of the business. Corporate thinks Regional Operations are cowboys that have no understanding of process and expose the organization to undue risk. Marketing creates materials that the sales teams ignore. Sales is always trying to circumvent internal processes and asks, "Do you want me to make sales or fill out paperwork?" Teams get into territorial pissing matches. The company promotes Collaboration as a core value, mostly because they suck at it.

One client I worked with had recently inherited a new team. When he sat down with each member of his new team, he discovered that one of the finance people on his team spent the majority of her time looking at the P&Ls of other teams. Her job was to figure out if some of their revenue should be on her team's P&L and some of her team's costs should be on another team's P&L. As he put it, "Her role delivered absolutely zero value to the company. Her only role was to move numbers around to make our team look better." It would be funny if it weren't so sad.

Another company I worked with had difficulty getting the technology team and the marketing and sales team to play nice together. The sales and marketing team was constantly talking to the customers and coming up with customized solutions that they would then ask the technology team to build. The technology team would be apoplectic that the marketing team had promised such a labour-intensive customized solution. The technology team would then build solutions that they would ask the marketing and sales team to sell, to which the response was, "Our customers don't want this!" The company's solution was to build a new Data Solutions Team that was half made up of marketers and half made up of engineers. This sounds like a smart solution, right? Bring the two groups together on the same team, involve the engineers in the sales process and Bob's your uncle. The only problem was that the engineers and the salespeople couldn't get along. Like putting dogs and cats in a room and closing the door. The team lasted less than two years.

Last example. I was coaching a Technology Risk professional who had received feedback that he was too black and white in his communication, negative and arrogant. Our first session together, he started off by saying he didn't need coaching on any of the stuff I had put in the proposal, he already new how to do all that, what he really needed help with was on what to do when someone ambushes you on a call with information they've clearly been hiding. I stopped him and asked why people who work for the same company as him would withhold information. "Oh, they're like the union, they think I'm there to get rid of their jobs." "Well, are you?" I asked. "No! If anything, I'm there to enhance their roles so they can focus on higher value work!" "And did you try telling them that?" Silence.

Different parts of the business not working well together is extremely common and does profound damage to the organization. It causes delays, time spent resolving issues, escalations, poor decisions and bad outcomes. You'll be picking up the theme here, but the solution is simple: communication.

- **Move people around**
- **Make "Put yourself in your audience's shoes" one of your core values**
- **Require escalation to be a joint exercise**
- **Encourage a culture of curiosity**

Move People Around

I had a client who worked for a major grocery chain. He was Vice President of Produce. He'd spent his entire career working in produce. His dad was a grocer and worked in produce. He grew up going down to the food terminals where all the trucks came in and people would haggle as the food came off the trucks. During the course of our coaching program, he was moved into a different area of the business, one that he knew nothing about. He found the change distressing, certainly out of his comfort zone. I told him that this was a good thing, an opportunity to learn another part of the business and an opportunity to develop his leadership skills outside of deep subject matter knowledge. It wasn't long before he was promoted to Senior Vice President. He was recently promoted yet again. His deep subject matter knowledge in produce was actually limiting. Moving him into an area he had no knowledge of forced him to open his perspective and rely on his leadership skills.

Moving people around in the organization gives people a different view and a different understanding of how the various groups contribute to the success of the organization. They do a better job of building relationships and collaborating, because they understand the perspectives and challenges of the different parts of the business.

Which leads directly to the next point:

Make "Put yourself in your audience's shoes" one of your core values

A lot of corporate values and behaviours make me roll my eyes and I'm not alone in that. "Innovation, Excellence, Collaboration, Respect, Diversity, Do the Right Thing" could be the values and behaviours of literally any company on the planet. They're just words. One organization I worked with went to great lengths to have simple, plain-language values and behaviours. The one I particularly liked was "Assume the other person has good intentions". How much conflict could be avoided if people heeded this advice?

I would add to this, "Put yourself in your audience's shoes." Promote this behaviour. It sounds so simple, and we know we're supposed to do it, but few of us ever do. We become entrenched in our view of the world. I was working with a VP of IT whose team was having conflict with another group from Strategy and Innovation. She and her counterpart had to get on a call with both of their teams to try to resolve the conflict. When I asked her about the call, she said "What they were proposing was a good idea, but it really doesn't fall under our current strategic priorities, and we don't have resources for it. So, as I said to my counterpart, it's not 'No', it's 'Not now'". I responded by saying, "Look, I don't know your counterpart, but if he's head of Strategy and Innovation, he's probably been brought in as a disruptor from some company like Google or Amazon (turns out he was from Google), and that hearing IT say innovation isn't a strategic priority simply served to confirm in his mind how backwards the organization is. He also probably didn't believe that this would be a priority the next year either. This will likely force him to go higher up to push for change because he and his team aren't getting any traction at the operational level." She paused and said, "That's probably exactly what he was thinking." The thing is, I just guessed all that from her counterpart's job title. Any of us can do the same simply by imagining ourselves in our audience's shoes. What are they thinking, and maybe more importantly, feeling? When you see something from the other side, finding ways to collaborate becomes much easier.

When I started out coaching in the late 90s, I think it's fair to say that HR wasn't overly respected. I constantly heard complaints that the training that was provided by HR was completely useless, because it didn't address the real world needs of employees. This was something I constantly had to overcome whenever I was brought in to do training – I knew that the majority of the people in attendance didn't want to be there and were anticipating a bunch of fluff. I cut my teeth convincing tough groups of the value of what I was offering. Today, I see a very different landscape. It's common practice for companies to have HR Business Partners. These are HR professionals who are embedded in the business and report to both HR and the senior leader in the vertical they support. This shift comes from a recognition that to provide valuable support, they need to truly understand their audience.

Require escalation to be a joint exercise

I've often described 'escalation' as a fancy word for 'telling', as in, "I'm telling on you!" When there's conflict, employees will often cc their manager. This leads the other person to cc their manager. Neither person looks good when this happens. When my children were younger and they bickered, they both got sent to their rooms. I'm often surprised how often employees go to their managers with problems. To my mind, part of being a professional is always presenting solutions, or at the least, options. Escalations are essential when two individuals or teams are at a stalemate, and don't have the authority to impose their solution. In this case, both parties need to come together to lay out the issue, why it's a problem and jointly put forward the options available. This is a much more mature approach, both parties look good, and it helps build trust. No one's trying to screw the other. Making teams and individuals work together before escalating will help build bridges, reduce the number of escalations, make escalations easier to resolve when they do happen, and avoid conflict between teams that can damage the organization and take time to repair.

Encourage a culture of curiosity

Another way to avoid conflict between teams is to encourage the asking of questions. When I work with clients, they often ask for coaching on how to answer questions. I've never had a client ask to get better at asking questions. I deal with the art of asking questions in the Listening section of this book, but it needs to be supported at an organizational level. When IT is having a requirements meeting with the business, are they simply trying to find out what functionality is required for what they are developing, or are they genuinely trying to understand the business' needs? Asking questions is often seen as weakness. If we are experts, then we should have all the answers. In fact, asking questions shows strength and openness. And you just might learn something you didn't know or gain a new perspective.

The better different parts of the business work together, the better the solutions, the less wasted time, the better the workplace environment. My entire career I've heard clients say that their organization is too siloed. I've seen the flattened hierarchy come and go. The reality is, companies have silos, or verticals, or business units, or whatever you want to call them. Employees have different expertise, different perspectives, and different priorities. Communication is the main tool to avoid the pitfalls that inevitably arise from this reality. Not only will a focus on communication avoid problems, but it will also help achieve those two elusive goals: improved productivity and engagement.

CHAPTER SEVEN

DON'T TOLERATE POOR COMMUNICATION

Every fall, friends of the family invite us over to pick apples. They have a lovely old orchard that produces an incredible harvest. Wandering through the orchard to find unbruised apples is one of my daughter's favourite annual rituals. But what to do with all the apples is always a challenge. After we've made sauce, apple crisp and everything else we can think of, there's always a full bin left over. This year, I was going through the apples and noticed that at the bottom, there was one stinky brown apple in the middle of a circle of apples that were starting to go bad. I pointed this out to my partner, and she looked at me, and explained, "Well, yes, that is why there's the expression 'It only takes one bad apple...'" My eyes widened. Fifty years old and I'd never really thought about where that expression came from.

Everything I've been talking about with communication works when everyone is trying to do it. But it just takes one jerk to ruin everything. My clients often want to work on strategies to deal with 'difficult people'. We work on many of the things discussed in this book, from looking at things from their perspective, putting forward arguments that address their issues, using positive, assertive language, etc. But the real answer is to get rid of the jerks. My role is to provide coaching to individuals to give them the skills and tools to succeed. But it's difficult for an individual to truly be successful if they aren't playing by the same rules as others. They need the support of the organization.

Robert I. Sutton wrote The No Asshole Rule in 2007. It's a good book, you should read it. My takeaways were twofold: develop a hiring practice that screens out assholes; fire the asshole.

An unhealthy communication culture sucks the life out of an organization. One asshole can corrupt an entire team. People are less likely to speak out, they are more likely to put themselves first, develop cliques, and mistrust management. Most organizations have some sort of internal policies around respect, diversity or inclusion. That's great. But if the organization doesn't walk the talk and actively promote and *enforce* those policies, it won't do a bit of good. Let's start with the simple stuff. No employee should ever be yelled at. No employee should ever need to confront racist, sexist, homophobic, transphobic, or hateful speech. Not even as a 'joke' – not funny. Any employees involved in such types of communication should be fired. No employee should be belittled or purposefully ignored. Employees engaging in such behaviour should be warned, with documentation, and if the behaviour continues, they should be fired. Employees shouldn't be allowed to be passive aggressive, officious or downright snotty. If they are, they should be spoken with, coached, trained, disciplined. If they can't or won't change their behaviour, they should be fired. There's a theme here: fire the asshole.

This type of egregious, negative communication is more common than you'd think. A few years ago, I was hired by an investment banking firm to provide leadership and communication coaching. If you visit their website, the first navigation tool directs you to their Diversity and Inclusion page which proclaims their guiding principle as 'Fostering diversity to create success for all'. After working there for awhile, it came out that the president was a notorious bully who would often make sexist comments in meetings. The board knew this. And did nothing. As a result, the workplace culture was incredibly toxic and anyone who could find work elsewhere did so. I worked with a client who had a Senior Vice President tell her she should stop losing so much weight because she looked like a cancer patient. I've worked at other companies where IT and the business would get into screaming matches. One company had an incident where a senior vice president ripped a phone out of the wall and threw it across a boardroom. None of these people were fired. They should have been. Firing the asshole gets rid of the asshole, lets other assholes-in-waiting know that the behaviour won't be tolerated, and most important of all, signals to everyone else that the company has their backs and is genuine when they talk about their Values.

Years ago, a client of mine used an expression that I like – What you Permit, You Promote. If you accept an invite to a meeting that has no agenda, you just told the person they don't need to have an agenda. If someone pings you during time you have blocked off to ask if you have a time for a quick chat and you say yes, you just told that person it's okay to interrupt time you have blocked off. If you respond to an email your boss sends you on a Saturday night, you just said it's okay to email you on Saturday night. If a direct report comes to you with a problem and you solve it for them, you just taught them to come to you with their problems. Promoting a positive workplace environment doesn't work if the organization doesn't enforce it. What you permit, you promote.

The organization needs to clearly communicate their expectations around communication culture, and it needs to hold everyone accountable. Here are a few suggestions:

- **Guidance on how to run effective, inclusive meetings**
- **Clear guidelines around unacceptable behaviour, accompanied by consequences**

Guidance on how to run effective meetings

Some years ago, I was working with a client who was the head of a global IT division. She was practically revered in the organization for her leadership skills. Her team was responsible for responding very quickly to outages or major events within their IT systems. When an event occurred, there would be an emergency call with upwards of 80 people spread out across the globe. She described these calls as high-pressure events and bemoaned the fact that certain people dominated the calls, often talking over or interrupting others. She said that she often didn't get a chance to hear from the people on the team she wanted to – mostly women and introverts. She said that she herself was often interrupted, despite being the most senior person on the call. She wondered if this was because she was a woman, with the double whammy of being in a highly male IT world and leading a global team with high cultural diversity. While this was likely a factor, the main issue was that there had been no ground rules laid out for these calls. I recommended she reach out to her counterparts who were the leaders of some of the people on the call to develop a set of rules for how to conduct the calls and how to solicit input from the participants. She and her peers then actively communicated the culture they wanted to develop and shared the meetings rules with their people. The difference was immediate. After the next call, she had a debrief with the Directors who reported to her. They couldn't believe the difference in participation and outcome and mentioned hearing from several participants who rarely ever spoke on the calls. All the people mentioned were women and introverts.

We often leave communication up to chance and hope that people behave well (or our definition of behaving well). Hope is not a good strategy. People need guidance. It's the easiest thing in the world for an organization to set forth its expectations and provide guidance for how to run effective, inclusive meetings. Which makes me wonder why it's so rare.

Clear guidelines around unacceptable
behaviour, accompanied by consequences
Every carrot needs a stick. Mmmm, carrot. Ouch, stick! I've talked about the need for organizations to promote a positive communication culture and to provide the tools and training to achieve it. This will help the majority of the people. There also needs to be clarity around what is unacceptable, and the

consequences of these things being ignored. This needs to be made clear during the hiring process, during the onboarding process and needs to be reinforced constantly in the organization. Many organizations have anti-bullying policies. Communication behaviours need to be explicitly spelled out within this, and there needs to be clear, documented HR policies to enforce it. I don't profess to be an HR expert, but there would likely need to be an explicit process that starts with a written warning, offers training or coaching, and culminates in termination. The first time an asshole gets fired for being an asshole, the organization will cheer. And will be healthier for it.

I worked with an organization that made a concerted effort to create a more collaborative, positive, work culture. They hired a firm that identified three types of culture: Green (passive defensive); Red (aggressive defensive); and Blue (constructive). The company did assessments for teams and individual leaders, introduced the Blue behaviours they were looking for and actively and consistently promoted Blue Culture. Of course, people would roll their eyes, and when people behaved poorly, employees would often sarcastically comment, "That wasn't very Blue Culture". But despite the cynicism, they now had a language to identify and call out the behaviour. The company had provided their employees with the tools to tackle bad behaviour. Changing culture is massively difficult. Employees, even senior leaders, can't do it on their own. Not even the CEO can do it. The organization as a whole needs to actively promote what is required. And when individuals do not live up to expectations, there need to be clear, visible consequences.

CHAPTER EIGHT

CREATE A CULTURE OF COACHING AND MENTORING RATHER THAN FEEDBACK AND EVALUATION

Many organizations have begun to incorporate coaching and mentoring as an official part of their HR policy. This is a good thing. I find coaching and mentoring to be a far more effective way of encouraging growth than feedback and evaluation – I would even argue it can be more effective than training. The problem is that feedback and evaluation are linked to compensation. By and large, feedback is given when there is a perceived problem or deficiency, and it is an attempt to correct the problem. Performance evaluations are a formal part of the manager/direct report relationship and can affect salary, bonuses and career progression. There is a power imbalance in these relationships, and they are not always well-received. And feedback can often have negative, unintended impacts felt for years after it is given.

Working 1:1 with clients, I often hear things other people don't. I have had so many clients relay feedback to me they have received, often more than a decade ago: "I speak too quickly. My voice sounds like a little girl's. I say umm too much. I fidget too much. I ramble. I come across as arrogant." Whenever I hear something like this, I always ask, "Did receiving this feedback fix the problem?" "Well, no, I tried to slow down for a few weeks, but I eventually just went back to what I always do." Telling people what they do wrong makes them feel bad about themselves. It creates anxiety that can actually impede their performance. It can make them feel defensive and erode their relationship with their leader. And there isn't always a direct correlation between the problem and the solution. Fixing a problem requires an understanding of its underlying cause and it requires trust from the individual trying to make the change.

Coaching and mentoring involve a much slower process. It takes time and commitment on the part of the organization. Coaching and mentoring helps employees understand what *to do* versus what *not to do*. Any idiot can tell someone what they're doing wrong. It takes someone with experience and commitment to help guide people to improve. Those of us that have been fortunate enough to have had mentors know how lucky we are. Good mentors are extremely rare – most of us only get a few in a lifetime, if we're lucky. But oh, what a difference they can make. A good mentor, a good coach, can change someone's life. But we often stumble upon them by happy accident. The organization needs to step in and play a role in coaching and mentoring.

- **Make coaching and mentoring a formal HR policy**

- **Stop training people on how to give feedback – train them on how to solicit feedback instead**
- **Make performance discussions a continuous conversation**
- **Use coaching and mentoring to improve delegation**

Make coaching and mentoring a formal HR policy

As I mentioned, many organizations already do this and there are plenty of consultants out there who are willing to help set up an internal coaching and mentoring program. I don't have much to add to the logistics of that. But what I would add is to make communication and leadership an active topic of discussion between mentor and mentee. I refer to communication as the invisible asset – it needs to be talked about, made visible, if an organization wants to tap into the power of a positive communication culture. Coaches and mentors are ideally positioned to have these conversations.

Stop training people on how to give feedback – train them on how to solicit feedback instead

I thought Douglas Stone and Sheila Heen's book Thanks for the Feedback was revolutionary. Essentially, it argues that companies should shift from providing training on how to give feedback, to training people on how to solicit and receive feedback. Most of us are familiar with the training new people leaders are given around how to provide feedback. It is colourfully and colloquially known as a 'shit sandwich' – the person providing feedback starts off by saying something positive about the person, then delivers the feedback in the middle and ends off with something positive – *as if the person receiving the feedback doesn't notice what's inside, because damn, that bread tastes good!* Okay, so this stuff isn't in the Thanks for the Feedback book, that's me. The reality is that people who are prickly and defensive tend to be that way regardless of how the feedback is delivered. In fact, if the feedback is delivered too nicely, it's often an excuse to avoid internalizing it.

What Stone and Heen found was that when people solicit the feedback themselves, they tend to be far more receptive. If they are provided guidance on how to receive, interpret and process feedback, they are able to show improvement far more often than when the guidance is focused on the giver of the feedback. In other words, we've been doing it wrong. Train people on how to solicit and receive feedback. It seems so obvious, and yet, most companies I work with still use their resources providing training to all new people managers on how to give feedback.

Make performance discussions a continuous conversation

People are awkward about feedback. So, we avoid it. Feedback tends to only happen when there's a problem, or semi-annually when there's a performance review. Both of these scenarios are heightened emotional situations. In the first scenario, when there's a problem, the receiver of the feedback feels like they're in trouble, and they often feel defensive or outraged. On the other hand, performance reviews are infrequent and have direct impacts on people's careers. Neither of these situations create the ideal atmosphere for having an open and productive conversation.

Feedback should be an ongoing part of a leader's interactions with their direct reports – and by feedback, I mean positive and negative. We need to be just as exacting when providing feedback around what someone does well if we want them to continue to do that thing well. Weekly one-on-one meetings should be used to provide ongoing feedback. Team meetings are also opportunities to have those discussions. Leaders are often encouraged to celebrate success in team meetings – agreed, but instead of "Great job!", try talking about specific actions taken or decisions made that linked back to the strategy, or that demonstrated the core values. Providing employees with direction, guidance and continuous feedback is essential to improving performance (and engagement and productivity).

It's also important to note that the strong performers on a team need just as much feedback as the poor performers (and are often more coachable). And yet, poor performers take up most of the leader's time. Someone who is struggling may get more time in their 1:1s or have more frequent meetings. They may be given a coach. And the strong performer, who *isn't a problem*, receives far less support. And yet, investing time and energy in supporting and developing strong performers is an investment in the future leaders of the organization.

Performance discussions between leaders and direct reports need to be a standard part of 1:1 meetings for all employees. Talk about performance. Talk about it in a mature, ongoing way. It's the only way it will improve.

Use coaching and mentoring to improve delegation

When an employee is newly promoted to a senior role, they are often offered an executive coach. One of the main things executive coaches suggest is that their client needs to delegate more. It makes sense – most people who are promoted are highly effective individuals who are accustomed to being on top of everything. Unfortunately, the characteristics that made them so successful can become an impediment at this level. They can't possible be on top of everything, but they still try, which slows things down, creates a bottleneck and makes the people below them feel micro-managed. Thus the "You need to delegate more" advice. I've had many clients that have been told this by their executive coach. And my clients tend to agree. But, as one client put it, "If they had the skills necessary to take this on, I already would have delegated it to them." This is where coaching and mentoring come in. I advise my clients to set a delegation target in the future – by X date, I want to hand this responsibility off to this person. I then suggest they create a coaching/mentoring workback plan to help the direct report get to the stage where they are ready to take on the new responsibility. This plan should be communicated to the direct report, so that they know what they are working towards. Delegation creates efficiency in the organization, it helps develop future leaders, and like everything else, it depends on a culture of good communication to be successful.

If companies spent less time on update meetings and reinvested some of that time into coaching and mentoring, we would see productivity and engagement increase. Coaching and mentoring helps people be better at their jobs. Creating a mature, positive environment that is focused on improvement gives people a sense of direction and accomplishment. Again, we see how focusing on a positive communication culture pays dividends.

CHAPTER NINE

BUILD SPACE FOR BOTH
INTROVERTS AND EXTROVERTS

I landed my first professional acting gig at age 18. When I was 24, I started coaching executives on presentation skills. I deliver dozens of speeches, workshops and training sessions every year. My entire career has been about speaking to people, often from centre stage with big bright lights shining on me. I'm also a hardcore introvert. In the small town where I live, my friends jokingly (maybe?) refer to me as a hermit. When I have been through an extra busy stretch of teaching or speaking, often traveling to do so, I need to retreat to my pottery studio, or hop in my canoe to recharge my batteries. Being an introvert has in no way hindered my ability to communicate in public. But as an independent consultant, I have had the latitude to shape my world in a way that suits my personality. Many people in the work environment don't have this freedom.

Introverts aren't inherently poor communicators. In fact, most of the best actors I worked with over the years were introverts. We're not disengaged or poor team players. But it can often look that way because the work environment places us in situations that reward extroversion. To understand what I mean, it's important to look at the definition of introverts and extroverts, both for what the definition is and what it isn't. Quite simply, an introvert likes to form their thoughts before speaking and it takes energy to be around people. An extrovert likes to form their thoughts while speaking and gets energy from being around people. That's it. It's not about being shy or outgoing. Introverts and extroverts can be equally successful in a variety of roles that would often be thought of as the other's domain. We just need to build space for both types to succeed.

Apparently, somewhere between 30-50% of the population qualify as introverts, which is a surprisingly broad range. Suffice it to say, we're in the minority. Functional areas like IT, Finance, Data Analytics and Audit often have the inverse ratio, with introverts being the dominant personality. Perhaps not surprisingly, I have spent much of my career working with these areas. Far more than Sales or Marketing or even Operations. Many introverts do a good job of pretending to be extroverted, but it takes a toll. We are often implicitly and explicitly told that we should be more extroverted – we should speak up more at meetings, we should enjoy team-building exercises, we should smile more (don't tell someone to smile more). But acting more like an extrovert isn't the answer. Not only is it taxing for us introverts and makes us feel like there's something wrong with us, but it also doesn't allow our strengths to shine through. Introverts are processors. We often think about things from all angles. We can be contrarians. These are all valuable traits. But we need to be put in the right kind of circumstance to excel. Going back to the actor example, extroverts are great at improvisation. Introverts love rehearsals to really dig deeply into the part. I wouldn't put an introvert into an improv show and I wouldn't cast an extrovert to play a love-stricken poet.

Because extroverts *like* to think on the fly, the hectic pace of communications can actually be a benefit. Extroverts are able to make comments in meetings, answer questions quickly and brainstorm ideas very easily. So, having a day of back-to-back meetings, conference calls, with e-mails and texts crammed in between doesn't present the same challenges to extroverts that it does for introverts. This reality can be extremely draining for introverts, but more importantly, it doesn't allow them to do their best work. And creating an environment that fosters the best work from all employees is in the organization's best interest.

There are some simple ways to create an inclusive environment for both introverts and extroverts:

- **Include Introverts and Extroverts as part of Diversity, Equity and Inclusion policies**
- **Change your interview process to include a written component**
- **Require substantive agendas for meetings**
- **Allow for flexible work schedules**
- **Institute best practice of follow-up emails for meetings**

Include Introverts and Extroverts as part of Diversity, Equity and Inclusion

I think the first step to creating an environment that plays to the strengths of both introverts and extroverts is to recognize the differing needs. Introverts often feel like they have to pretend to be someone they're not. I was coaching a very smart and successful Managing Director of Mergers and Acquisitions at a large bank. He came to me because he wanted to get better at small talk. I asked him to describe an example. The first example was a networking evening for his university alumnae program that he felt compelled to attend. He went, felt awkward, had some stilted, polite conversations with a few people and then snuck off when he felt he'd stayed long enough to be seen. The second was a seasonal work party. He attended because he felt it was important for his team that he be there and because he wanted to have a quick talk with the group President in an informal setting. After he'd accomplished both objectives, he made up a lie about his children being sick and his wife having a big presentation the next day so that he could leave early. My coaching was simple. Don't go to the networking event. You suck at it, you're busy, you don't like it and you never will. For the second event, I told him that what he did was fine. He had a purpose for attending, planned out the conversation he wanted to have and then left. That's what introverts are good at – planning and thinking things through. Done. Easiest coaching gig ever.

As introverts, we are often made to feel ashamed for not enjoying the things we're supposed to. Much of my career has involved traveling to deliver training and keynote speeches. Well-intentioned clients often invite me for dinner or drinks with the team. They're just trying to be nice and make me feel included. For years I would either go and be dying inside or make up an excuse as to why I couldn't come. I even developed the habit of booking the earliest flight home so I could avoid having to share a taxi with a client, or God forbid, stay an extra night and have dinner with them. One day, after I'd been doing this for 20 years, I was staying with a large team at a resort (extrovert thinks – fun!, introvert thinks – trapped!) and my contact invited me to dinner with the group. Again, she was just trying to be nice. For the first time ever, I responded, "That's very kind, thank you. I'm actually quite an introvert and spend my whole day talking, so I like to use my evenings to recharge in my room." She shrugged her shoulders and said, "Okay, makes sense. Have a nice night!" She didn't care. So why had I spent the past twenty years pretending to be someone I'm not?

By including introverts and extroverts in the Diversity, Equity and Inclusion policy, you will be formally acknowledging and creating room for difference. This will give both introverts and extroverts permission to articulate their needs.

Change your interview process to include a written component

As a theatre director, I saw hundreds, if not thousands of auditions. I auditioned many introverts and extroverts. Extroverts tend to do well in auditions – they are personable, outgoing, quick to accept direction. Introverts sometimes struggled with these elements – particularly in the ability to quickly understand a directorial suggestion and adapt their audition piece on the fly. This is an important part of an audition. The director wants to see how well the actor can respond to direction. But what I learned is that if I cast the extrovert, what I saw on opening night would be very similar to what I saw in the audition. If I cast the introvert, they would use the rehearsal period to work, think, process and improve and by opening night there would be a very different performance. But the audition process doesn't reward introversion. Had I instead given the actors direction and then asked them to come back the next day, it might have given me a more accurate understanding of the actors.

So, why do we base most of our hiring practices on live interviews where the applicant doesn't know the questions in advance? One of the classic characteristics of an introvert is that we will think of the perfect thing to say twenty minutes after a meeting has ended (because we are still processing it). But the interview process doesn't reward this. It rewards thinking on our feet and responding on the fly. Hiring practices should include both a written and an oral component. And I don't mean the cover letter. I mean a series of written questions that the applicant can complete in advance of the interview. Because introverts like to form their thoughts before speaking, this will level the playing field and provide companies with a far better means of gauging the strengths and weaknesses of applicants.

Require meetings to have a substantive agenda

Having a proper agenda should be mandatory for any meeting, but it is especially important for introverts and extroverts to work effectively together. I was working with a marketing team for a telecommunications company that was neatly divided down the middle between extreme introverts and extreme extroverts. They were having a hard time working together and it was generating frustration and conflict. At one point during a session I was teaching, one of the extroverts asked the introverts, "What's one thing that I could do that would help?" One of the introverts in the room immediately blurted out, "Have an agenda!" Given that introverts like to form their thoughts before speaking, having a substantive agenda will allow them to enter the meeting prepared, helping them to participate more effectively. The key word in that sentence is *substantive*. Even when meetings do have agendas, they are often standing agendas that lay out the flow of the meeting, or they are a list of topics to be discussed. A good agenda will clearly articulate the point and the desired outcome of the meeting. This will allow all participants (especially the introverts) to come prepared and will help the meeting be shorter and more focused.

I have often worked with leaders who express frustration that certain people on their team don't participate and wonder about their level of engagement. I usually suggest that they follow up with an email asking the individual if they have any thoughts on what was discussed. Often, they will receive a thorough and well thought out response. The people leader's response is often, "This is great – I wish you would have said this in the meeting!" Had they been provided with a substantive agenda in advance, they might have had time to prepare and contribute more effectively.

Allow for flexible work schedules
For years I prided myself on being a workhorse. I could fly across the continent, work long days, meet with clients at any

time, on top of raising a family, taking care of the house and maintaining a creative life. Until one day I couldn't. I was fried. Fried from years of pretending to be a high-functioning extrovert. A few years ago, I started implementing a practice I would never have dreamed of earlier in my career: I don't book clients after 3:00. I would have been ashamed, think I was sending the wrong message, maybe I'd never work again! But then it occurred to me that my clients pay good money to work with me. After 3:00, I'm functioning at about 60%. Given the choice, would my clients prefer to have me today at 60% or wait a day or two and get me at 100%? It made perfect sense to me. But it took me more than 20 years to get there.

The corporate environment can be particularly stressful for introverts. Given that it takes energy for introverts to be around people, a day filled with back-to-back meetings can be a significant drain. This doesn't give the introvert time to recharge, to process, to strategize or to think through problems. While an extrovert might want to talk through a problem, an introvert will want some quiet time to think about it. Both approaches work, but if there is no balance, introverts will be at a disadvantage. It can lead to low engagement and eventual burnout.

Companies need to create an environment that is designed to get the most out of their employees. I am currently working with an organization that has moved to ROW – Results Only Work. Doesn't that sound grown-up? Like, do your work, get the results, we're good. Don't do the work, don't get results, you're fired. Why do I care if you do it between 9-5 with fifteen-minute breaks and an hour for lunch? Sure, employees need to be available for meetings, but this sounds like a much more mature way of approaching professionalism. Allowing for flexible work schedules will allow introverts to plan their day in a way that will work best for them. The pandemic normalized flexible work schedules – this is a practice that needs to be continued, regardless of the future of the workplace.

Institute best practice of follow-up emails for meetings
In-person communication is essential to coming to a place of agreement. Meetings aren't going away, and they are an integral part of the workplace communication culture. But when introverts and extroverts work together, there can often be confusion as to what was agreed upon. Introverts often like to process their thoughts. If they haven't spoken up in a meeting, their silence can often be misinterpreted, when in fact they simply need time to form a response. Likewise, an extrovert may often say something, or have an idea in the moment that they aren't really attached to or move on from very quickly. But other people in the room might take something they said quite seriously (particularly if the extrovert in question is the leader). This confusion simply arises from the different ways of thinking/speaking of introverts and extroverts. After a conversation or a meeting, it is always a good idea to follow up with a quick e-mail laying out what was agreed upon in a few simple bullet points. Not only does this create a paper trail, but it also helps to avoid confusion and conflict.

SECTION TWO

BUILD YOUR INDIVIDUAL COMMUNICATION SKILLS

Even if an organization only does some of what I suggest in the first section of this book, it will have achieved an important goal: it will make communication top of mind for everyone in the organization. This is half the battle. Part of why I see so much poor communication is that people don't even think about how they're communicating. They open their mouths without thinking. They attend meetings without preparing. But the other part is that they need to learn how to communicate well. Most people don't try to be bad communicators. But even when they are aware they need to improve, they often don't know how. And if nobody else is doing it, then they have very little incentive to improve, and very few models to emulate.

The guidance that people receive around communication is often bad. People are told they speak too quickly. So, naturally, they try to slow down. Which makes them sound like William Shatner, isn't how their brain works, and they revert back to what they've always done. Clients are often told they need to be more succinct. Because they don't know how, they arbitrarily cut content, which might make it a little shorter, but no clearer. A new leader will often tell their team they want them to put everything into one slide. So, the team shrinks the font size and crams everything into that one slide. Teams are always talking about 'the story we're telling in this presentation', but no one really knows how to make a presentation a story, and even if they do, it becomes long and winding. The line between recognizing a problem and solving the problem isn't always a straight one. In fact, simply highlighting the problem sometimes make it worse. Individuals need good guidance on how to be good communicators.

If we're going to set the expectation of good communication, employees need to be given the tools and the support to do it. Good communication doesn't just happen by accident. Individuals need training, templates, and positive examples. Good communication begets good communication. Bad communication begets bad communication. If someone sends me a rude email, I respond with a rude email. If someone sets a positive tone and creates a safe atmosphere, I will be more open and collaborative. There needs to be a tipping point where good communication becomes the norm. And while the organization has a huge role to play in this, it is ultimately up to the individuals doing the communicating to make it all work.

Communication is a skill. We often think of it as a personality trait. Some people just seem to be naturally good communicators. A number of years ago, I was working with a group of CFOs (I don't know why they had more than one) at an insurance company. I had asked each of them to prepare a short talk and then deliver it to each other. As we went around the room, I have to confess the talks were all varying degrees of boring. Except for this one guy. His was great. So, I asked the others what had made his talk stand out. There was a moment of silence around the room before one of his colleagues piped up: "That's just so-and-so. He's a natural." The others sagely nodded their heads in agreement. I said, "Hold on. Is his DNA sequencing different from yours? He's doing stuff. And the stuff he's doing is what made his talk so good. So, what was he doing?" There was a pause. "Well, he started with a story." Then someone else jumped in, "He used very conversational language. No finance jargon." "Okay, what else?" "His arguments were really clear, and he put his main point upfront." The conversation went on as the group identified more and more things that had made the talk so good. Once you identify the things that make communication successful, they then become repeatable. And repeatable things are things that can be learned. And things that can be learned are skills.

The following chapters are a set of practical principles to help individuals improve their communication skills.

CHAPTER TEN

TREAT ALL COMMUNICATION AS A LEADERSHIP OPPORTUNITY

Communicating as a leader is a mindset as much as anything. It's a decision. About a year into the pandemic, I was coaching an individual who worked for a large outdoor clothing brand. I would begin every session we had by asking what had happened during the previous week, if he had applied the things we'd been working on, what his thought process had been as he went through his days filled with meetings, emails and presentations. About halfway through the program, he described a presentation he had been on the receiving end of. He said, "The presenter did everything you say not to do. She was leading a new enterprise-wide software implementation, and her presentation was a pure information dump, there was no engagement at all. I thought if she had put her thesis upfront, even if she had included three or four things our team could be doing to prepare for implementation, it would have been so much better. There are things our team is doing she probably wasn't aware of. It would have started a conversation. I'm just wondering if you think I should provide her with that feedback?" I responded, that sure, he could give her feedback, depending on their relationship it may or may not be well-received. But then I asked, "At the end of the presentation, did she ask if there were any questions?" "Yes." "And were there any?" He laughed. "No, total crickets. I don't think anyone was paying attention, we just wanted it to be over." To which I responded, "Well, couldn't you have asked, 'What are three or four things we could be doing to prepare for implementation?'" He slowly put his head in his hands. Because it wasn't his presentation, and it wasn't a particularly good one, he wasn't engaged and missed an opportunity to provide leadership. Then I said, "There is nothing I can teach you to make you ask that question. Skills and tools and tips and techniques won't make you ask that question. That's a decision about how you show up to a meeting, how you engage with your colleagues. Leadership is a decision, and it's a decision you make or don't make a thousand times a day."

As an individual's career advances, they often spend less and less time doing what they were trained to do and more and more time communicating. I was working with the head actuary at an insurance company recently and asked him when the last time he did any actuarial work was. Real math. He responded, "About a decade ago. I mean, I have to understand the numbers to participate in meetings, but I haven't done any actuarial work in years." Communication doesn't just become part of the job – it *is* the job. Most leaders spend their entire day in meetings. If their job is to be leaders, and their days are spent almost exclusively communicating, then how they communicate is how they lead. If A=B and B=C, then A=C. Communication is leadership.

Most people don't treat their daily communication as leadership opportunities. Sure, if they have a big presentation to the board, or to the executive committee, then they prepare, go over their notes, show up ready to deliver. But the weekly standing update meeting? Their 1:1s with direct reports? Their project team meetings? Mostly, they just show up. I'm mostly pretty nice to my clients, but I tend to be hard on this point. If you are attending a meeting, you are prepared. If you can't be prepared, you shouldn't be there. A few weeks ago, a potential client reached out to ask about my small group training sessions. She had invited her leader to the call, as it would be the leader who would ultimately make the decision. The woman's leader had her camera off for the first part of the call while I talked about the importance of always being prepared, about it being the true mark of a professional. When she turned her camera on, it became clear she was eating a sandwich and reading the course description I had sent the week before for the first time. We waited for her to get up to speed, asking questions around her sandwich that had already been answered in the email exchange she had been cc'd on. Given my preamble about leaders always showing up prepared, it was a little awkward. I didn't get the work.

How we show up sets an example to others. It is a sign of respect. It also *saves time*. In the above example, had the woman's leader showed up prepared, the meeting would have been half as long. She would have already thought of relevant questions. Instead, she wasted our time. Many years ago, I attended a theatre workshop for a play in development.

A young playwright/director had invited many prominent theatre artists to the workshop performance. It wasn't very good. Afterwards, the young artist was speaking to a very well-respected writer and performer who was giving him some pointed criticism. The young artist was becoming somewhat defensive and responded, "Well, it was just a workshop." To which the more senior artist responded, "No. It was my precious time." A bit harsh, perhaps, but I bet that young artist never forgot it.

I constantly have clients ask me what they can do to get more engagement from people on their calls. I somewhat snarkily respond that they should stop wasting people's time, be interesting, and the group will be more engaged. It's not like the people on the call are playing Wordle. They're probably replying to emails because they decided it was a better use of company time than paying attention to the meeting. If we treat every single communication as a leadership opportunity, all day, every day, then we will get the most out of our day, the most out of our interactions. We will be more productive and more engaged. And as much as shifting our approach is a mindset and decision, there are two practical habits we can develop that will help:

- **Shift your thinking from expert to leader**
- **Always show up prepared**

Shift your thinking from expert to leader
For about a decade, I taught a course called Speaking as a Leader for an organization I worked for. It was one of those expensive corporate courses at a lavish resort that leaders flew into to attend. I would always start off the course by saying,

"Hi. My name's Simon. You've all signed up for a course called Speaking as a Leader. Which suggests to me that you're not currently speaking as leaders. Why else would you be here? But I checked your job titles, and you are all leaders. So, if you're not currently speaking as leaders, what are you speaking as?" I'm sure they were all thinking, "Who is this charming, quirky, handsome young fellow?" Eventually we would talk about it and the response would be that they were speaking as experts. Which makes sense. For the first half of our careers, it is our expertise that is valued. When we are invited to speak, it because we're a subject matter expert (a SME!). And that is what we learn to value in ourselves – our knowledge. I then asked a follow-up question. "If you were to assign a verb to the objective of someone who is speaking as an expert, what would that verb be? In other words, what are they trying to do when they speak?" We would go Family Feud style through verbs, and the top three were invariably: Inform, Educate, Explain. I then followed up by asking them the same question regarding speaking as a leader. The verbs were very different: Inspire, Influence, Convince, Persuade, Motivate. Which one would you want to listen to? Whose meeting would you like to attend? The thing is, being an expert and being a leader are not mutually exclusive. Companies need their experts to be persuasive, inspiring, and influential. It's my belief that our intention should always be to lead, regardless of our position in the organization.

The simplest way to do this is to shift focus from the subject matter to the audience. Instead of simply asking what the meeting or presentation is about, ask "Who is it for?" Always start with the audience, rather than the information.

Ask yourself, "What is the one single idea I want everyone in the meeting to walk away with?" We lead people, and to do that, all communication has to start with the audience.

Always show up prepared

Preparation is the mark of a professional. I'm a big sports fan, and while sports analogies in the corporate world tend to be tired cliches, I'll try this one on you. My two favourite teams are the Toronto Maple Leafs and the Toronto Blue Jays. I've always been a sucker for punishment, and these two teams offer plenty of that. These days, both teams have incredibly talented young players who are really fun to watch. And both teams have brought in veteran athletes to stabilize the dressing rooms and act as mentors. On a number of occasions, I've seen the up-and-coming young stars being asked what they value in the veterans' presence. All the answers are essentially: "The rigour they bring to their preparation. Every day it's the same. They prepare the same way, win or lose, whether it's the first game of the season or the last. They teach us how to be professionals." Talent and hard work can get a young person to the show. Rigour and habits are what make them professionals. I would argue the exact same thing is true in all professions.

I coach my clients to do one simple thing. At the end of each day, I ask them to look to the next day's calendar and prepare a mini outline for each of their meetings. This outline includes a few simple elements:

- What is the one point I want the attendees to walk away with?
- Why should they believe it?

- How can we do it?

I ask them to do this, even if it isn't their meeting. I was recently delivering a component of a leadership development program for a company. One component of the program was that the participants would have half hour mentoring sessions with various leaders in the company. One individual remarked on the difference between two of the leaders he met with. One showed up on the call and they had an interesting, if meandering conversation. The second showed up prepared, with notes. My client couldn't believe how much they were able to accomplish in that half hour call. Not to mention how respected he felt that the senior executive had taken the time to prepare for their call. Good leaders prepare. It's not reasonable to think that we're just so darned smart that we can show up at a meeting, get up to speed and offer the perfect input. Good leaders don't lead by the seat of their pants, and that means being prepared.

While good communication is indeed a skill, it needs to start with the right mindset and the right preparation. Treating communication as a leadership opportunity demands preparation. Imagine an organization of employees all showing up to meetings prepared, and ready to step up as leaders. Imagine what could be accomplished. While you're imagining that, let's move on to the brass tacks of how to do it.

CHAPTER ELEVEN

STRUCTURE YOUR THINKING

I coach executives for a living. Most of them are fairly polished by the time they get to me. They're clearly good at what they do, have been in the business a long time and have received a reasonable amount of training over the years. So, when I ask them what their objectives are for the coaching program, they will often respond, "I want to ensure that whenever I speak, the audience gets my message." I say, "Great! That's what I do!" Then over the course of our conversation, they'll mention they have an upcoming presentation or townhall. I'll say, "Okay, what's your message?" And they talk for ten minutes. And I'll say, "Sorry, what was your message? That was a gist. A bunch of stuff." Here's an obvious point: in order for the audience to get your message, you need to have one. And maybe more importantly, you need to be able to articulate it in a single sentence. Most people can't. They can't in meetings, they can't in presentations, they can't in emails, and they can't when answering questions. There's a lot of talk about conveying the message, but not a lot of clarity about what that message is.

Now, I use the word 'thesis' rather than 'message', as I find message is over-used, often suggests 'spin' and can mean different things to different people. Thesis is clear. It is the single idea you want to convince your audience of. There's no point building a slide deck, or starting an email, or opening your mouth to answer a question if you don't actually know what your point is. And yet, most people do exactly that every single day. Think about it. After watching a presentation, if someone who wasn't there were to ask you what they missed, you would likely distil it down to one sentence – "Well, things are going pretty well, but we really need to put more focus on our value-added services." If the audience is going to distil it down to one sentence anyway, why not do it for them? They're more likely to walk away with the point you want them to if you do.

I believe the main reason I see so much pointless (literally) communication is that we are speaking as experts rather than leaders, and as such, we gravitate towards sharing information rather than communicating ideas. Most people start with the content and then try to walk the audience through it. I see this everywhere: after the engagement survey, HR will report findings (63% of those surveyed feel we collaborate well), sales teams report numbers (new activations dropped 23% in Q3), marketing reports on KPIs (click-through rate dropped 38% after promotion ended), IT provides milestones (project moved to testing phase). It's a lot of fancy-sounding Show and Tell. Companies spend an enormous amount of time pumping out information. Unfortunately, when we walk the audience through content, we are leaving it up to them to figure out why they should care about the information. And if there is a main point, it is typically delivered at the end.

Structuring your thoughts is actually quite simple when you start with the audience rather than the information. There are two steps to structuring your thoughts:

- **Develop your thesis**
- **Develop arguments that convince the audience of the thesis**

Develop your thesis

Knowing what your point is isn't as easy as it sounds. Sometimes there is no clear point to the content. Or the point is ambiguous. Shifting your focus from the content to the audience can help clarify your point. It allows us to shift from *telling* the audience something to *convincing* them of something.

A few years back I was coaching a Vice President in the legal department of a major bank. There had recently been federal legislation passed that would require banks to only recommend products to customers that were in the customers' best interest. The legislation was in response to call centre employees being caught trying to sell products to (mostly elderly) customers that they didn't need, sometimes costing them thousands of dollars. My client had been asked to speak to a group of business leaders about the upcoming legislative changes. "The problem is, they want me to tell them what they need to do to be compliant with the legislation and my answer is 'Well, it depends', which is what lawyers always say and they don't want to hear that." I suggested he look at it a different way. "If there was one idea you would like the business leaders to walk away with, what would that idea be?" He thought about that for a moment, then responded, "Well, that if we tackle this the right way, it could give us a competitive advantage." "What do you mean?" I asked (my job lets me ask all sorts of smart questions.) He explained that when he was working in private practice, his firm had a similar experience with online retailing legislation. His firm had both eBay and Amazon as clients. He said that eBay sent in a list of issues they had questions about relating to compliance. "They wanted to check the boxes and keep the legal bill to a minimum." Amazon, on the other hand, flew a couple of their lawyers down to their headquarters, put them in a boardroom, while a series of business leaders passed through and grilled them with questions about the legislation, trying to find a competitive advantage. "I'm not saying that's why Amazon rules the planet and eBay has floundered, but I sure noticed a difference in approach. I think we could be faced with the same type of situation." "That's perfect," I said. "Tell that story, then deliver the thesis that if approached the right way this legislation can offer the bank a competitive advantage, give a couple of reasons why and then close by asking them to reach out to your legal team."

When asked to deliver a talk about the content, he couldn't think of a thesis. When he shifted his focus to convincing the audience of an idea, the structure flowed easily and naturally. This is a perfect example of shifting from information to ideas.

Develop arguments that convince the audience of the thesis

Once the thesis has been developed, the structure is usually quite simple. There are only two questions in the English language that convince anyone of anything: Why should I believe you; How can we do it? All the other questions (Who, What, When, Where, How Much) provide supporting information. They aren't the structure of the argument. So, over the years, I have taught my clients three structures and three structures only.

The Why structure is used when you want to convince the audience we *should* do something. The outline is simply a thesis followed by a list of reasons why the audience should believe the thesis. I've worked with IT departments my entire career, and after working with them for awhile, I realized that half their presentations were essentially the same:

Thesis – We need to invest in replacing the legacy infrastructure.

- (Why?) The current infrastructure no longer serves the needs of the business
- (Why?) We're holding the infrastructure together with binder twine and duct tape
- (Why?) The cost of maintaining the legacy infrastructure is increasing exponentially
- (Why?) The current infrastructure presents a security vulnerability
- (Why?) There's a fully scalable off the shelf solution that would meet our current and future needs

What I like about this example is that the fact the company is holding the infrastructure together with duct tape suggests that people have been unsuccessful at convincing the executives to make the investment in the past. I know why. I've seen those presentations, filled with dense, technical information. Sometimes the more we explain something, the less persuasive we become.

The How structure is used when you want to convince the audience we *can* do something. It looks the same as the Why structure, except that instead of answering the Why, it answers the How. At the beginning of the pandemic, I saw the How model being used a fair bit.

Thesis – We can successfully pivot to online delivery.

- (How?) We need to provide employees with the tools to work from home
- (How?) Our website needs to be upgraded to allow for ease of online ordering
- (How?) We need to aggressively market the pivot to our customers through social media
- (How?) We need to partner to increase our delivery capacity
- (How?) We need to provide enhanced protection for workers delivering curbside pick-up

No one had to be convinced of why it was a good idea – everyone was locked down in their homes. They needed to be convinced of how it could be done.

The third structure is what I call an If/Then – this is commonly used for updates or presenting problem/solution situations. Here would be an example of an update:

Thesis – We need to make a concerted effort to get this project back on track.

(Problem) Everything's going to hell in a handcart.

- (Why?) The vendor sucked so we fired them
- (Why?) Our business partners don't know what they want so the scope keeps changing
- (Why?) Half the team is down with Covid

- (Why?) We're already behind schedule and over budget
- (Solution) We need to press restart.
- (How?) We've retendered the RFP for a new vendor.
- (How?) We need to sit down with the business to have a visioning/requirements conversation
- (How?) This will give us time for everyone to get healthy again
- (How?) We need to halt all expenditures and rework the project plan for executive approval

Each of these structures were achieved by asking four simple questions:

- What does the world look like through my audience's eyes?
- What's the one idea I want them to believe?
- Why should they believe it?
- How can we do it?

These four questions can help structure your thoughts for any communication for the rest of time.

One last story. I was working with a company that had a gating presentation for any new product launch. These were very stressful for the people presenting because everything hinged on a successful outcome to this presentation. Teams spent weeks building the slides, adding stuff, removing stuff, changing the order. After I'd already seen three or four of these presentations, I finally got a little antsy (okay, cranky). I asked my client, "Who is the audience?" "Ummm, the marketing executives?" "Right, what do you need to convince them of in this product launch presentation?" Big pause. "That the product's ready to launch?" "Right, there's your thesis. Why should they believe that the product is ready to launch?" "Well, that we've done our market research, the pricing is appropriate for the target market, we have good collateral materials to support the launch, the sales team has received the right training, and we have good KPIs in place to track the launch." "Good there's your structure. Now you just need to provide data to support each of those points."

Yes, the presentation will hinge on having the right data to support the arguments, but the structure is established, and the data now has a clear purpose. Not only did it only take about thirty seconds to hammer out a structure they had been working on for weeks, that structure will apply to all future product launch presentations. Just by starting with the audience.

Having well-structured thoughts is the key to all good communication. The little outlines described in this chapter can and should be used for all communications. When you get in the habit of structuring your thoughts before communicating, it becomes part and parcel of who you are as a professional. It also helps you take advantage of the leadership opportunities all around you, just by focusing on convincing the audience of ideas rather than sharing information.

CHAPTER TWELVE

BUILD YOUR OWN STRATEGIC COMMUNICATION PLAN

All leaders in an organization have strategic objectives. They have KPIs attached to those objectives to measure their team's progress against the objectives. The leaders develop plans and timelines to achieve the objectives. They build budgets and assign resources to the objectives. Everything they do is about achieving their strategic objectives. But do they have a communication plan to help them achieve those objectives? Nope. And yet, communication is at the heart of achieving anything. Teams need to understand, and hopefully believe in the strategic objectives. Different parts of the business need to work together effectively. Client groups need to buy in. Executives need to sign off. All of which hinges on good communication. And yet, again, the one glaring omission in all this planning is a strategic communication plan.

Many years ago, I was working with the SVP of a financial institution. He had been tasked with solving a problem that had been plaguing the organization for years – they had 17 different call centres for their various lines of business, each using their own platforms and processes that reported data differently. You would think this would be a slam dunk. It's painfully obvious that the executives need to see the same data reported the same way to be able to compare apples to apples when making decisions. Moving to a common platform and set of processes would streamline operations, ostensibly saving money and time. The CEO had even made an official decree to make it happen. And yet, every other executive who had been assigned the task had failed. The question my client asked was, "Why had they failed?" The answer he came up with was that the people in charge of the call centres didn't want to lose control. So, he approached the leader of one of the business units, someone he knew was reasonable and likely the most easily convinced. He said, "Look, I want you to have the head of your call centre report to me dotted line. She can still be solid line reporting to you. I want her to sit in with my team and we're going to help make your call centre more efficient and save you money. The only thing I ask, is that if I deliver on my promises to you, you need to help me sell the solution to the other business unit leaders." It worked. Within a year, he had managed to get all 17 call centres onto one central platform, all dotted line reporting into his team. What did he do that his predecessors had failed to do? He had a strategic communication plan.

Building a strategic communication plan should be an essential beginning of year activity for all leaders within the organization. Here's how to build a strategic communication plan:

- **Identify what big picture success looks like**

- **Identify key stakeholders for each objective – Who do I need to convince of what?**
- **Build elevator pitches**
- **Communicate at every conceivable opportunity**

Identify what big picture success looks like

There is a definite difference between operational thinking and strategic thinking. Operational thinking tends to be head down, firmly rooted in the present. A number of years ago I had a client who was a senior director in IT who was being groomed for an executive role. He was universally loved and admired for his commitment, intelligence, and work ethic. But he lacked strategic vision. Thinking it was a lack of opportunity, his leader assigned him as the lead on a huge project for the organization called The Store of the Future. It was a high-profile project that would allow my client to stretch his strategic muscles. When we first met, I looked at a preliminary presentation he had put together on the topic. Apparently, the store of the future was the store of the present, but without any of the problems they currently had. Operational thinking tends to focus on solving problems, which, don't get me wrong, is an incredibly important skill. But strategic thinking moves beyond solving problems to picturing what big picture success looks like.

Another client had recently been put in charge of the company's franchise division. When I asked him what a healthy, high-functioning franchise model looks like, he answered, "Sure, XXX$ EBIT per square foot." Nope, that's how you'll know you have a healthy franchise model. What does good look like? "Oh, well, good is when we have engaged, happy franchise owners who are committed to the strategy. If you have that, the rest of the plan should fall into place."

Once you have a vision of what you're working towards, you have to bring everyone else along.

Identify key stakeholders for each objective

Stakeholders are people who hold a stake in something, right? People who have an interest or a concern in something. People. Every strategic objective has stakeholders attached to them. These people usually fall into three categories – up the organization, down the organization and across the organization. For each strategic objective, the leader should make a list of the key stakeholders. The people in each of these groups need to be convinced of something if an objective is going to be achieved. One of the most important questions a leader can ask themselves is, "Who do I need to convince of what?"

I was working with the head of a customer service organization for a telco who described his team's challenges. He said, "My team ends up being the mop up crew for the organization. Our job is to get the NPS (Net Promoter Score) up. So, we go in, work with the customer. And we do a pretty good job of it. But if we didn't have so many low NPS scores being thrown our way, it would free the team up to focus on higher value work to help us achieve our objectives. The problem is that we can't control the fact that another team is sending us all these unhappy customers." So, his team couldn't focus on their strategic objectives because of the actions of another team. After we talked about it, my client reached out to his counterpart who led the team sending the low scores his team's way. They figured out a way for their teams to work more closely together, so that both teams could better focus on their strategic objectives. Despite the fact his counterpart wasn't in his direct chain of command, the success of each of their objectives were dependent on each other. They each had a stake in the other's success.

Build elevator pitches

Once the key stakeholders (or, People Who Need to be Convinced of Something) have been identified, I coach my clients to create short elevator pitches, like the outlines showed in the previous chapter. They should look like this:

Stakeholder – Partner team – Technology Risk

Thesis – Despite being responsible for different lines of defense, our teams need to work closely together.

- (Why?) Joint responsibility for oversight
- (Why?) Save time to reduce duplication of effort
- (Why?) Identify and respond to risks more quickly
- (Why?) Create more accurate reporting for board
- (How?) Assign one delegate to each other's weekly meetings
- (How?) Proactively communicate issues
- (How?) Share resources when possible

An outline like this should be created for each of the stakeholders identified. I encourage my clients to keep them in line of sight, even on a whiteboard in their office. It's very difficult to achieve anything without good, consistent communication and having the elevator pitches visible will help keep this top of mind.

Communicate at every conceivable opportunity
Much of good communication is repetition. Not just mind-lessly saying the same thing over and over but being able to link abstract ideas to concrete reality.

One of my clients was the head of a nuclear power agency. He was new to the role and wanted to instill a new culture of accountability in the organization. Whereas before, there was a culture of blame, he wanted to create a safe environment, where people felt comfortable taking and owning accountability. I pointed out that 'culture of accountability' is one of the most overused phrases in the corporate world, and it was going to take a lot more than talking about the new culture at an offsite. He was going to have to talk about it every day on their morning safety calls. He was going to have to model the behaviour and repeat the mantra over and over if he had any hope of changing things. One day, God only knows how, the plant sent out an erroneous emergency Tweet that there had been a nuclear incident. People that lived in the area started evacuating as panic started to spread. After a few hours, a communication was sent out that the Tweet had been an error, there was no incident. I wondered what the 'culture of accountability' looked like on the call after that debacle. Did people feel comfortable taking and owning accountability? Or did heads roll? If they were able to work through the incident maturely, then the message would be truly instilled. If people looked to apportion blame and heads rolled, then all that communication would go out the window. Good communication is hard work and needs to be absolutely consistent. This is the job of the leader.

Achieving strategic objectives is the primary goal of senior leaders. It's what they're paid to do. But it's not the senior leaders who actually do the work to achieve those objectives, and their teams aren't working in a vacuum. The only way to successfully achieve those objectives is to get people pointed in the right direction and working well together. And having a strategic communication plan front and centre sure helps.

CHAPTER THIRTEEN
MANAGE YOUR CALENDAR

If something is worth doing, it's worth doing right. And if you can't do it right, don't do it. There's a lot of half-assed communication going on out there – verbal diarrhea emails, people showing up unprepared to meetings, half-listening to presentations while they respond to emails. Given the importance of communication, it needs to be treated as, well, important. That means preparing for all your meetings. But preparation takes time, time most of my clients don't have. About a year into the pandemic, one of my clients said, "I miss airplanes. I miss my morning commute." Not because he enjoys being stuck in traffic or sitting at O'Hare airport as the flight is delayed once again. "I miss having time to think. Time when no one can get hold of me. I used to use my morning commute to go over the day ahead and plan. Airplanes were for getting work done." Not that using your morning commute to plan for your day is necessarily a healthy practice, but at least it was *something*. When people started working remotely, meetings flooded in to fill up that space.

Part of the reason there's no time to prepare for meetings is that we don't prepare for meetings. When we get onto the hamster wheel of running from meeting to meeting, we're in constant react mode, which is inefficient. Meetings take longer to get to the point and are less likely to produce solid outcomes. There's more back and forth with emails because of a lack of clarity. Taking the time to do communication right the first time actually saves time in the long run. But it requires stepping off the hamster wheel.

There's an old adage when doing DIY home renovations that you should always measure twice and cut once. I remember being in a Home Depot late one Saturday and seeing a fellow behind me with a single 2X4. I said, "Didn't measure twice, huh?" He nodded ruefully and smiled. Because he hadn't taken the time to make sure the measurement was correct, he ran out of wood and had to go all the way across town to get another 2X4.

The same principle applies to communication. I was working with a client a few months ago who described a situation that had recently happened. Her team was one of several providing updates on an executive call. Her team had less than favourable numbers, but they were largely caused by another team's lack of execution. After they'd shown these numbers on the call, the other team was upset, feeling that her team had thrown them under the bus. She said that it had taken three follow-up meetings to work things out with the other team, calm the waters and figure out a path forward. How hard would it have been to have a half hour call with the other team prior to the executive call to talk through what they were going to present? Not only would it have been respectful, helped build the working relationship between the teams, it would have saved two and a half hours of trying to undo the mess that had been created through a lack of planning and proactive communication.

If we are going to use good communications to be more effective, then we need to take the time to plan. To do that, we need to actively manage our calendars. And we need to be militant about it.

- **No agenda? No meeting**
- **Block time to think and stick to it**
- **Assign time for replying to emails**

No agenda? No meeting

When I work with clients, I will often ask them to share their screen to look at their calendar. Usually, at least half the meeting titles include the words 'Touchpoint, Alignment, Sync Up or Update'. This is lazy double-speak, for "I just want to slap something in the calendar." It's actually a form of procrastination. They don't have time to deal with whatever the issue is, but by putting a meeting in your calendar for next week, they feel they're doing something. In other words, you're paying for their lack of planning. I strongly encourage clients to decline, or at least push back on meetings with no agenda. A polite way of doing this is by replying with something like, "I noticed you booked an hour in my calendar. I actually only have a half hour. If you could send me your thoughts on what you'd like to accomplish in the meeting, I can make sure to come prepared so as to make better use of your time." It's polite, but firm.

If you look at your calendar right now, I'm going to guess that a lot of the meetings in it are a) unnecessary b) too long and c) have too many people invited. Meetings take up the bulk of my clients' time, so if we're looking for opportunities to increase productivity (or just stay more sane), look no further. If you have direct reports, make sure that they have an agenda for all your meetings. Whenever you request a meeting with someone else, make sure to always have a clear, substantive agenda. Building rigour around your meeting schedule sets an example for everyone. People will be more engaged because they know why they're there and will feel their time is being used well.

One of the simple ways to wrestle your meetings under control is to set a target for yourself. If you currently spend an average of five hours a day in meetings, devote four hours. If that number is seven hours, reduce it to five. This is one of the simplest ways to use communications to improve productivity and increase engagement.

Block time to think and stick to it

You simply can't be performing at the level you're capable of if you don't block time to think. A lot of people do their actual work at night, after their day of meetings. This leads to burn out and is unnecessary. By tightening up your meeting schedule, you can use that time for thinking. When we are in react mode, we often find ourselves fighting fires. Fighting fires takes up more of our time. But the fires are often the symptoms of some bigger or deeper problem. Giving ourselves time to think allows us to use our time more wisely, and to start working proactively rather than reactively.

Now, many of my clients do in fact block time in their calendars. And they let it be whittled away. A direct report will see the open time and send a quick note saying, "Hey, do you have time for a quick chat?" Wanting to be nice, my clients will often say, "Sure, of course." And that quick chat turns into 20 minutes. And they've just implicitly told their direct reports that it's okay to interrupt the blocked-out time.

We also have endless distractions in the form of all the various communication channels – Teams chats, texts, emails, and an endless stream of Yammer, Slack and who knows what else. Focus time needs to be just that – focus time. Turn off your notifications. Or hey, get up from your desk and go for a walk. Whatever it is you do, you need to get yourself out of the vicious cycle of communication and that requires commitment on your part.

Assign time for replying to emails

When I ask my clients how many emails they receive a day, the answer is often, "Over two hundred." Not all of them need to be responded to, but many do. When I ask them how much time they allot to responding to emails in their calendar, the answer is usually, "Zero." Just to be clear, when we don't allot time to responding to emails, we are de facto planning to not have enough time to do our jobs. Or we're planning to respond to emails in meetings instead of paying attention, which means we are probably doing a crappy job of both.

Of the two hundred or so emails, usually five or six need some thought put into them. It usually takes about five to ten minutes to draft a proper email, sometimes longer. That's an hour a day that should be devoted to this form of communication. Of all the companies I've worked with over the years, there were two that had a company policy of blocking time to respond to emails – one was a utility company, and one was a tech company. I've never had clients that responded so promptly to emails.

Given that communication takes up most of our time, we need to be judicious in how we engage. If we want to be more effective in our roles, more in control, we need to be incredibly rigorous in how we manage our calendars. It truly is the first step to being more complete professionals.

CHAPTER FOURTEEN
BE SUCCINCT

Get to the point.

No, sorry, there's a little more to it than that (though, not much!)

Blaise Pascal famously wrote in the margins of a very lengthy letter, "I have made this longer than usual because I have not had time to make it shorter." Clarity is the basis of brevity and clarity requires the time to properly formulate your thoughts. Up until this point, most of the recommendations I've made have been around taking more time to prepare for communications. This section is on how to be more succinct in the communications themselves.

Alongside developing executive presence, becoming more succinct is one of my clients' top objectives. Typically, the client is transitioning into a more senior executive role and where before they may have had ten or fifteen minutes to get their point across, they now need to articulate it to other senior executives within a minute or two. This is easier said than done. While people may know they need to be more succinct (Be bright, be brief, be gone!), they don't know how to do it. The approach most people adopt is they try to boil their content down, to condense it.

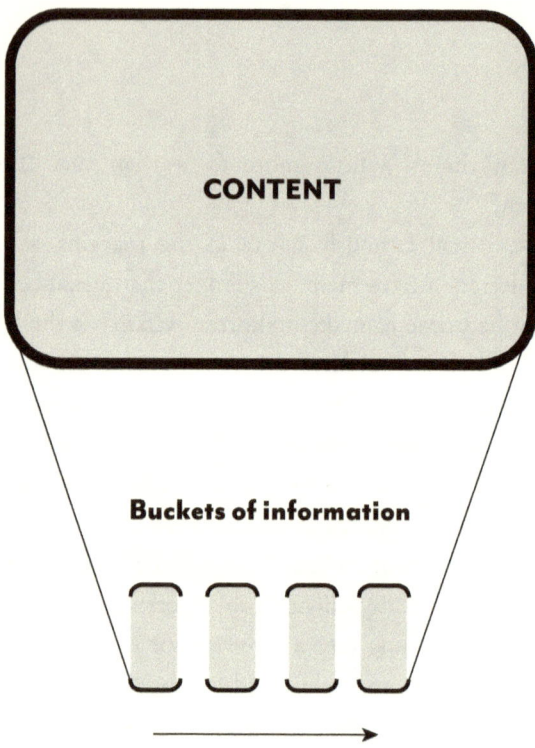

Buckets of information

This makes perfect sense to the speaker. The audience doesn't have any background or context for what they are hearing, so the speaker walks them through the content in order to explain. There are several problems with this approach. It's confusing for the audience and easy to lose the plot. And it's almost impossible to be succinct with this type of approach. The audience needs to be walked through the content and if it is too high-level or has had too much content removed, it won't make sense. Another big issue with this type of approach is that the structure is defined by the content, meaning that the structure will be different every time. But the biggest issue is that there is no audience in this approach. We constantly forget about the audience. When someone is asked to present, they usually ask, "About what?" and "How long?" Often, I will look at a client's calendar and ask about a meeting. The title of the meeting will usually be the subject – Marketing Campaign Strategic Alignment or some such. But when I ask who will be on the call, they often don't know – they have to click on a different part of the meeting invite to see the participants and often that part is overlooked. But communication is all about the audience. And therein lies the key to brevity.

- **Make audience-focused arguments**
- **Prepare bullet points for meetings**

Make audience-focused arguments
For a number of years, I worked with a large telecommunications company. They had a CEO who was notoriously impatient when it came to communications. One SVP I was coaching quite earnestly asked me what to do when the CEO holds his hand up an inch away from your nose to shut you up mid-sentence. So, when a VP was asked to provide the CEO with an update on a technical issue, he did everything he could to make the e-mail he sent as succinct as possible. He put everything in bullet points. He removed any extraneous information. When it was finally as succinct as he could make it, he pushed send and went to bed. The next morning when he got up, there was already a response from the CEO in his inbox. It said, "Too long – didn't read." The VP had two take-aways from this experience. The first was that the CEO was just being honest. When he thought about it, he realized that he often did the same thing – didn't read an e-mail – he just didn't tell the person who sent it. The second take-away

was that the reason the e-mail was too long, despite his best efforts, was because he had been trying to explain the issue to the CEO, rather than putting the main idea the CEO needed upfront and supporting it with a couple of key points. As long as his intent was to explain rather than to convince, it would never be succinct enough.

To be succinct, you need to start with the shortest version possible and then add content where needed, rather than the other way around. The way to do this is to start with the audience. What is the one single idea you want the audience to walk away believing? There is no point opening your mouth, or building a deck of slides, until you know what that point is. Start with a single sentence. Then put yourself in the audience's shoes and ask yourself, "What arguments would convince me of that one single sentence?" By asking yourself these questions, you build the short outline described in the previous chapter, with a single thesis followed by supporting arguments. At that point, you can look at each individual argument to see what data or content would be required to substantiate the arguments. Rather than boiling content down, this approach inverts the triangle by starting with audience and the single thesis. It looks like this:

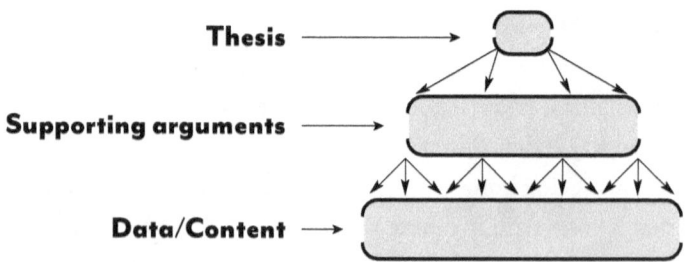

Thesis ⟶

Supporting arguments ⟶

Data/Content ⟶

The goal is to persuade your audience rather than educate them. This allows you to place your main idea (thesis) up front, followed by the structural arguments that, when put together, will convince your audience of your thesis. This gives you control over the length of your talk: you can deliver it in 60 seconds, 5 minutes or an hour, depending on the depth of detail you go into to support your structural arguments.

Learn to think in bullet points

Learning to think in bullet points is harder than it sounds. If a communication is an information dump, or a rambling explanation, there really isn't a logical structure, or the thinking behind the structure is unspoken. That's why so many PowerPoint slides have such long bullet points – they aren't really arguments, they're highlights, or points along the journey. A lot of the bullet points I see are sentences with a few words removed. A good bullet point should be 5-7 words long, with a verb in it. Once you shift your approach to convincing the audience rather than explaining or informing, it is much easier to prepare bullet point notes for yourself in all situations. This will help you be more succinct.

I was conducting a group session a few months back and I was checking in with each of the participants around what they'd been working on. One of the participants, a VP of technology explained that he had previously booked an hour-long meeting with a counterpart to discuss an issue. He hoped to convince his counterpart to adopt a different solution to the issue, one that would benefit both their teams. The VP said that in advance of the meeting, he prepared the thesis, (that he believed the solution he was preposing would benefit both their teams), followed by several bullet-point reasons underneath. He said the meeting was super simple, they both agreed, and in the end, only took twenty minutes rather than an hour. It took him all of ten minutes to craft the bullet points for the meeting but shaved forty minutes off the meeting itself. Sometimes, you might even find after crafting your bullet points that you don't even need a meeting, that an email would suffice. More time saved. If you take time to craft a few simple bullet point arguments for all your meetings, you will find you're able to get to the point more quickly, provide clarity and guidance and get better outcomes.

Being succinct isn't just making your content shorter. It's a product of clarity. We ramble when we don't really have a clear idea of what we're trying to say. Clarity of thought should be at the heart of all communications – brevity is the end result.

CHAPTER FIFTEEN

DON'T LET POWERPOINT
TAKE OVER

This past year, I had a 1:1 session with an SVP for a tech company. Our session was booked for 9am Monday morning. After chatting for a bit, I said, "Your company uses a lot of PowerPoint, you must have seen a lot of presentations last week." He laughed. "You have no idea!" Then I said, "So, it's first thing Monday morning. Out of curiosity, how much do you remember from those presentations last week?" He sat silently for a moment, cocked his head to the side, looked at the ceiling, then said, "Nothing. Maybe a few key dates, but that's it." Now, granted, I heard he was let go a few months later, but the point still stands. An enormous amount of time and effort goes into building an awful lot of PowerPoint, and to what end? They are often forgotten moments after the presentation is done.

The topic of how much PowerPoint sucks has been done to death. Everyone laughs about Death by PowerPoint. I've been teaching PowerPoint since you used to have to print it off onto clear plastic transparencies and put them on an overhead projector (true story!) and people complained about it back then. So why hasn't it gotten any better? I would suggest the real problem lies in a combination of sloppy thinking and an intent to educate the audience rather than convince. This results in two symptoms, which are deadly to PowerPoint: noun clusters for slide headers; information dumps with the point at the end of the presentation. These issues are more difficult to resolve than simply telling people to use pictures and avoid too many wordy bullet points.

Many years ago, I was working with a client on how best to use Power Point. I was doing my thing, teaching her to put a single idea at the top of the slide, rather than a subject header. She responded that she had already been taught this approach, but that the instructor she learned it from had gone one step further and recommended using 'vertical and horizontal logic'. I asked what that meant. She explained that the vertical logic was what I was saying, that someone should be able to randomly pull a slide out of the middle of the presentation, read the top line and immediately understand how the content in the body supports the top line. The horizontal logic meant that someone should be able to pick up the presentation, read only the top line of each slide and understand what is being argued in the presentation. Brilliant. Who wouldn't want a presentation to be that clear and logical?

In fact, PowerPoint presentations can be extremely effective if a few simple principles are followed:

- **Make a point at the top of each slide (vertical logic)**
- **Embed your structure in the presentation (horizontal logic)**
- **Create a skeleton before building the slides**

- **Introduce the slide before transitioning (a little magic trick)**

Make a point at the top of each slide (vertical logic)
The biggest problem with most of the PowerPoint I see is that the header on each slide is almost invariably two or three nouns: P&L YTD; Gap Analysis; Critical Challenges; Audience Demographics; Customer Migration Rate, etc., etc. When the slide has a noun cluster at the top, the speaker is forced into information dump mode; they have no choice but to walk the audience through the content on the slide. If there is a point to be made, it is typically delivered verbally.

The solution is quite simple: place a short sentence at the top of the slide. This will ensure that each slide has a point. For it to be an active argument, there needs to be a verb in the short sentence. The rest of the slide is then freed up to prove or support the point that is at the top of the slide. The basic idea is this:

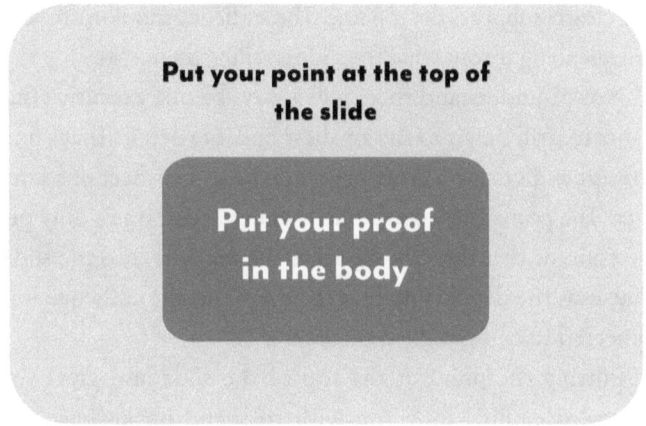

PowerPoint is most effective when the supporting content is presented visually. One of my biggest pet peeves is cut-and-paste Excel spreadsheets or tables embedded in slides. Tables are a completely agnostic way of presenting data – they tell the audience nothing about the data. Often you will see a Finance person presenting a table and several of the numbers are highlighted in red, or are bolded, because the presenter is trying to draw the audience's attention to these numbers. They are fighting the format of the table. Instead, try using graphs that have an inherent visual logic to them. For example, a line graph is typically used to show a trend. I was looking at a slide awhile back that had a line graph with a huge spike on one of the months. My eye was immediately drawn to it, because *that's what the presenter wanted me to look at it*. Had that number been presented in a spreadsheet, it would have been buried and difficult for the audience to figure out what they were supposed to see. Likewise, if you show me a pie chart, I will immediately look at the biggest piece of pie. A slide works best when the content is visually presented in a manner that clearly supports the top line. The audience shouldn't have to struggle to figure out what the slide is telling them.

Now, I understand there will always be one executive that wants to drill down to the smallest possible detail. That's fine. The appendices are a great place for the spreadsheet of source data. The point isn't to arbitrarily cut content, it's to only put the content that directly supports the top line into the slide. That way, the detail is there if required, but the audience isn't subjected to being walked through it all.

Putting the point at the top of the slide also gives you control over how long you wish to spend on it (have you ever been told you had 20 minutes to present and when you showed up, they asked if you could do it in 5? Of course you have.) As soon as the slide goes up, the audience should be able to grasp the point and how the body supports it. It's up to the speaker to choose how long to spend on the supporting detail. A recent client, a VP of Data Analytics for a grocery chain, said, "This is great! I'm going to test this when my direct reports send me a slide. If I put it up and can't figure out in 10 seconds what the slide is trying to tell me then it's not clear enough." Perfect. Now, reduce that to 5 seconds.

This was perfectly illustrated to me in a pair of slides I used to see regularly at some of the tech companies I worked with back in the day. The first slide was titled 'Current Architecture'. Underneath was a reasonably simple diagram, with a building on the left, an arrow leading to a cloud (representing a network) in the middle, another arrow to a cylinder (which represented a PBX), down to a set of mainframes, over to another building and back into the cloud. This slide would generally take the speaker five or six minutes to explain. Once they were finished explaining, they would transition to the next slide, which was titled 'Proposed Architecture', which, I could swear, was the same slide. Except, that after five or six minutes more explanation, a dotted red line appeared alongside the final arrow leading back to the cloud, at which point, we learn that the *current architecture runs the risk of data loss on the final leg of the journey* and the *proposed architecture ensures data integrity through a secondary pipeline*. Did you notice how fast that was? If the first slide had been titled 'Current Architecture runs risk of data loss' and there was a big red circle around the final arrow leading back to cloud and the second slide was titled 'Proposed Architecture ensures data integrity through secondary pipeline' with a big green circle around the dotted line next to the final arrow, those two slides could be presented in thirty seconds instead of ten minutes.

Embed your structure in the presentation (horizontal logic)

A client recently asked me to provide feedback on a presentation he had been asked to review. I started laughing the moment he opened the file. "What's so funny?" he asked. The first line read: 'Executive Summary (Slide 1 of 3)' followed by an entire slide of lengthy, dense bullet points. If the Executive Summary is three slides long, I don't think I want to know what the rest of the presentation is like! Another pet peeve is Executive Summaries that bear no structural correlation to the rest of the document. They're basically just a bunch of key highlights put in bullet points. When using vertical and horizontal logic, you can ensure your executive summary is reflected in the structure of the presentation. If someone reading the Executive Summary wants to dig a bit deeper into a specific point, they can flip to a slide with the same title as the bullet point.

The key to using horizontal and vertical logic in your presentation is in building a concise, idea-driven agenda slide. The agenda slide should contain your thesis and supporting arguments. This allows you to then place each of your supporting arguments at the top of the following slides, wherein you can use the body to support the argument at the top of the slide. Your agenda slide becomes your executive summary, and the rest of the presentation simply offers support, proof and validation for each of your arguments.

So, for an example, let's use the mini-outline I used earlier:
Thesis – We need to invest in replacing the legacy infrastructure.

- The current infrastructure no longer serves the needs of the business
- We're holding the infrastructure together with binder twine and duct tape
- The cost of maintaining the legacy infrastructure is increasing exponentially
- The current infrastructure presents a security vulnerability
- There's a fully scalable off the shelf solution that would meet our current and future needs

Let's translate this into a full presentation:

- Slide 1 – The topic of the presentation (Legacy Infrastructure), likely a standard internal template with company logo and pretty picture of happy people.
- Slide 2 – The Agenda – thesis, followed by the list of five arguments (see above).
- Slide 3 – Your first argument at the top of the slide– The current infrastructure no longer serves the needs of the business. In the body of the slide there would likely be three columns: Business Requirements; Current Capabilities; and Gaps.
- Slide 4 – Your second argument at the top of the slide– We're holding the infrastructure together with binder twine and duct tape (maybe change the language). In the body, show historical patches and customization on infrastructure.

- Slide 5 – Your third argument–The cost of maintaining the legacy infrastructure is increasing exponentially. Support with a bar chart showing year over year the increasing cost and time committed to maintaining the infrastructure.
- Slide 6 – Your fourth argument – The current infrastructure presents a security vulnerability. The body of the slide would likely show an historical timeline with last security update having been performed in 2017.
- Slide 7 – Your fifth argument–There's a fully scalable off the shelf solution that would meet our current and future needs. In the body, show a solution and how its scalability meets current and future needs.
- Slide 8–Repeat your thesis and present the action you are requesting of the audience. The action could be several asks, depending on where the audience is at: approval for the new solution; permission to further explore the solution and present back; invite sales team for proposed solution to present to IT, etc.

The horizontal logic ensures that someone could pick up the presentation, read only the executive summary and understand the argument. If they want more detail, they can flip to the corresponding slide. It is easy for the audience to understand and navigate. But the key to it all is building an outline first.

Create a skeleton before building the slides

I was talking to an SVP of a sales organization in New York who put the issue perfectly. He said, "Yeah, we tend to build the presentation first, then try to figure out what we're saying." I couldn't help but laugh, because it's so true. A bunch of people submit slides that then get cobbled together into a presentation, at which point someone calls a meeting, because 'we need to figure out the story we're telling'. Too late. Now you've got a mess on your hands. Never mind then sending the deck out for everyone's comments. Building a deck of slides collaboratively can be one of the more frustrating experiences known to humankind. Slides are moved. Slides are cut. Content is added. Pictures are added. And removed. Is the deck getting any better? Maybe, maybe not. But it sure takes a lot of time!

Even slides that I've seen that do have the point at the top were typically done backwards – the person created the slide, then tried to figure out what the point was and put it up top as a 'key takeaway'. A much better approach is to create a skeleton first. Figure out what the thesis and supporting arguments are before building the slides. If several people are building content for presentation, have a meeting where everyone agrees on the structure first, then have people take away individual slides (that already have the argument at the top) to populate. This approach not only creates a better end product, it also saves an enormous amount of time. And given the amount of time that goes into creating endless slide decks, the time saved from this approach, if applied across the organization, is significant.

I recently received an e-mail from a client with the subject line: 'OMG!!!!!! That was so easy!!!!!' He's the CIO of a financial institution who has to provide quarterly updates to the senior leadership team on the data analytics group's progress. Typically, this involves a week of back and forth with the person building the presentation for him. When we talked about this approach, he said, "You're right, I know what I want to say. I run the division." This time, he built a skeleton outline with the thesis and structural arguments on the agenda slide, followed by slides with the arguments on top and a circle with 'Insert Relevant Data Here' in the body. The person building the presentation inserted charts that supported the top-line arguments and sent it back to him. There was a little bit of back and forth, but in the end, they were able to finish the presentation in a single day.

Introduce the slide before transitioning (a little magic trick)

One of the biggest problems with how we use PowerPoint is that presenters put themselves in a no-win competition with their own material. Typically, a presenter transitions slides and then begins talking. From an audience perspective, as soon as the slide changes, we start reading the new slide, trying to figure out what it's all about. If the speaker is talking while we are reading the slide, we maybe half listen to the speaker, half read the slide. Except that the speaker is talking about the first point, and we are reading the third. If the slide is especially dense, we will often *actively shut out the speaker so that we can figure out what the slide is saying.* In either case, the speaker is in competition with his or her own material, and it isn't a competition they can win. The audience will always gravitate to the visual first.

By creating vertical and horizontal logic, we create a separation between idea and supporting content. This creates the possibility of a division of labour between speaker and slide. Human beings are good at speaking ideas (preferably with conviction) and PowerPoint is good at presenting proof (preferably visually). Having the idea at the top of the slide and the proof in the body allows for the division of labour to happen.

So, here's the magic trick: introduce the next slide before you transition to it. When you are at the end of one slide, introduce the single sentence at the top of the next slide, and then click the button. The audience hears the idea from you, while their focus is on you. Then the slide transitions and they look at it. They see the single idea at the top of the slide that you just spoke (most people will think, 'Oh, look, he was right!') and then will look to the body and see that the body supports what you just said. This gives you a chance to pause and check your notes before beginning to speak. While you are collecting your thoughts, the audience has a chance to look over the slide. You are now putting the ideas forward, PowerPoint is backing you up and you are controlling the pace of the presentation. The difference this makes in establishing your authority has to be seen to be believed. It is night and day what a difference this simple shift can make. All you need to do is prepare your notes so that you know what is coming next and practice introducing the slide before transitioning. Easy-peasy.

We've all seen the horrible ways PowerPoint can go wrong (no, you shouldn't turn your back to the audience, read the bullet points and use a laser pointer to repeatedly circle a diagram). But suggestions for improving PowerPoint often focus on the symptoms rather than the underlying causes. If your thinking is clear and well-structured, PowerPoint can be an exceptionally powerful tool. The trick is in embedding horizontal and vertical logic into the presentation and creating a separation of labour where the speaker is presenting the ideas and PowerPoint is providing the proof. Next presentation you build, make a quick outline for yourself before beginning: what's your thesis and what are your supporting arguments? Once you have those in place, building the presentation will be simple.

ANSWER THE DAMN QUESTION

I was sitting across the table from the President and CEO of a large financial institution. I had been hired to help him improve his ability to respond to analyst questions during earnings calls. I was a bit nervous, because you never know exactly how a CEO is going to respond to direct criticism. They can be prickly. And, truth be told, I often only understand half of what they are saying when I listen to earnings calls. So, I passed him the transcript of the Q&A section of the call and asked him to read one of the answers he had provided to a question. He read the passage thoughtfully, then looked at me and said, "I didn't answer the question, did I?" I breathed a sigh of relief and said, "No, that's what I thought, too." It's obvious when we read the question and the answer on the page after the fact, but in the moment, it's quite common for a speaker to miss (or avoid) answering the question. We then moved in to discussing how to make better use of the opportunity presented by the questions being asked.

Questions provide you with an incredible opportunity to persuade. In fact, I would suggest they are your greatest opportunity. There's a lot riding on how you answer a question. The way you answer a question will often retroactively determine whether or not the asker accepts anything you have said prior to the question. And yet, the Q&A is often a complete blind spot. I was helping a company that sells large laboratory tech equipment to hospital networks on their sales presentations. These are huge multi-million-dollar sales. Once we had worked on their PowerPoint and rehearsed presenting, I asked, "Okay, now how do you prepare for the Q&A? Do you practice throwing questions at each other, do you have a record of past questions?" They stared blankly at me for a moment, before answering, "We don't." What's the likelihood of making a multi-million-dollar sale without the prospective customer asking a question or two?

Likewise, I do a lot of work preparing the Investor Relations teams of companies for earnings calls and investor days. In a Rivel Research study, they found that while 80% of analysts cited the Q&A portion of the call as being of high importance (the highest ranked portion of the call, even more so than review of the strategy), only 41% of analysts responded that companies do a good job of answering questions. And yet preparation for the Q&A portion of the call is often fairly minimal, and even then, the preparation is usually defensive in nature.

Regardless of whether it is an earnings call, a sales presentation, a townhall or a team meeting, the answer to a question provides a huge leadership opportunity. But answering questions well is an art and requires practice. You need to prepare for the questions beforehand and prove a well-structured answer.

- **Prepare beforehand**
  - » **Want the questions and challenges**
  - » **Anticipate what their concerns will be**
  - » **Prepare your thesis**
- **Provide a well-structured answer**
  - » **Listen to the question**
  - » **Pause**
  - » **Give the answer and bridge to thesis**

Prepare beforehand

Want the questions and challenges

Okay, so this sounds a little fuzzy, but the mindset you bring to your preparation is essential. Many (most) of my clients have a defensive attitude towards questions and challenges. Sometimes they have a downright combative attitude. They talk about deflecting the question, defending their position, offering rebuttals. And it is true that sometimes the person asking the question can be aggressive or seeking to discredit the speaker. It doesn't matter. You need to embrace the challenge and genuinely want to know what the audience's concerns are. There is no way to capitalize on the opportunity a question presents if you have a negative mindset.

At the outset of my career, I had the opportunity to work with a large global mutual fund company that had been struggling. They had a new CEO who was taking questions at a townhall – except the questions were scripted and everyone knew it. When they were wrapping up, the facilitator asked if there were any more questions, knowing there wouldn't be. Except there was – one guy with his hand waving around like Horschack on Welcome Back Kotter (okay, that one was for the old people like me out there). It was awkward. They couldn't really ignore the guy, so the CEO, pointed him out and said, "Yes?" The question the individual asked was, "Well, you've been talking about all these great things we're going to do, but I'm just wondering why you think you're going to be able to accomplish them when no one else has in the past?" You could have heard a pin drop. The CEO laughed, then thought for a moment. "Fair question. I think because I'm stubborn. I believe in the strategy that's been laid out. And I'm stubborn enough to stick to it, even when things get hard, as they inevitably will." The answer went on for awhile, but that was the gist of it. A number of employees I spoke with over the years that followed told me that the moment when the CEO answered that question changed their feelings about the whole company. Some even said that it was the answer to that question that began the company's turn around. The real danger is that the question goes unasked, leaving you no opportunity to address the concern.

Anticipate what their concerns will be
Really being able to anticipate questions involves putting yourself in your audience's shoes and asking yourself, "What would I want to know if I was in their place?" We all know we should put ourselves in others' shoes, but we rarely do it. When we do put ourselves in the audience's shoes, it's usually quite simple to anticipate their concerns: we don't have budget for this; they're overstepping their territory; my team's already too busy to take this on. This perspective needs to be the starting place for your preparation. Ask yourself, "What are the top three or four issues I think might be concerns for

the audience?" You won't necessarily know the exact phrasing of the question, but by and large you know what the issues will be.

Prepare your thesis
Once you have identified what the issues will be, construct a single sentence that you want to convince them of about each issue. If you walk into a scenario where you will be facing questions, regardless of whether it is a job interview, a presentation or meeting, and you have three or four sentences that address the key issues, you are well-prepared. Typically, when I work with an Investor Relations Officer, they will have prepared a twenty- or thirty-page Word document prior to an earnings call with bullet point answers for every single question that might get asked. Sometimes when I listen to the webcast, after an analyst asks a question, I can hear the flipping of pages in the background as the executives search through the document for the answer. This causes me to do a facepalm. The analysts don't want a scripted answer. The longer Word document is a valuable exercise, but the next step is to create a single page document listing the key issues and the single sentence thesis you want to convey about the issue that has been raised. Coming up with the main point is much more difficult than providing a couple of supporting arguments.

A few summers ago, there was a huge container ship stuck in the Suez Canal. You might remember. It was kinda funny, if the ramifications weren't so huge. I was working with a client who was the COO of a large company who had a board meeting coming up. He didn't know what the exact question would be, but he knew the issue of the Suez Canal would be raised. I asked him what one idea he would like to convey to the board if and when the issue came up. He thought about it for a moment, then said, "Well, if anything, this issue validates our supply chain strategy." Perfect. It's not reasonable to think we will be able to come up with the perfect high-level thesis in the moment. That's what you want to prepare, and the rest will come from listening to the question.

Provide a well-structured answer

Listen to the question

Well, that sounds obvious, doesn't it?! I have spent hours upon hours reading through transcripts of Q&As and e-mails and I often find that the person didn't really answer the question that was being asked. Sometimes this is because the speaker is actively avoiding answering the question, but often the question itself is convoluted, or multi-pronged and it is clear the speaker simply stopped listening before the question was finished. If you've ever listened to an earnings call, you'll know that analysts only ever ask three-part questions. It must be part of their training. The reason we often miss the question is that we start forming our answer before they have done speaking. This displays the underlying intention of the speaker: either to show they know the answer, or to try to avoid saying the wrong thing. I would much rather they focus on providing the person asking with something of value. When someone is asking a question, you need to really listen to the question, fully and deeply, so that you not only understand the question being asked, but also why they are asking it. Only then can you really provide a good answer, one that capitalizes on the opportunity embedded in the question.

Pause

If you really listen to the question right through to the end, you will need a moment to collect your thoughts. A pause doesn't have to be long. But most of us start talking immediately, as if the question were a fire that needs to be put out. Or we say, "That's an excellent question" in an effort to buy time. Unless you're willing to call out a question as being incredibly stupid, you should probably avoid commenting on the quality of the question. The problem when we start talking immediately is that it causes a separation of brain and mouth. I am talking, but my brain is furiously racing forward to try to figure out how to make it all add up. This forces a structure where the speaker comes to the main point at the end of their answer, when in fact it should be at the beginning. Give yourself a moment, even half a second, to collect your thoughts.

Give the answer and bridge to thesis

A well-structured answer is accurate, concise, clear and honest. The true art of answering questions well lies in the speaker's ability to answer the question directly and then bridge to the thesis.

This should happen in the opening two or three sentences. The first sentence is the opener, and it should directly address the question as it was posed. This means answering the question as clearly, directly and succinctly as possible. If the question is a yes/no question, the first word out of the speaker's mouth should ideally be 'yes' or 'no' (I often can't quite believe I am paid to tell this to CEOs and CFOs). A clear direct answer in the opener establishes credibility and is really the price of admission for the rest of the answer. This opening creates the opportunity to then bridge up to the big picture thesis that the company or individual would like to communicate about the issue raised in the question (which, hopefully, was anticipated and prepared for). After the opener and thesis are delivered, two or three supporting points can be presented to support the thesis. These are usually reasons why the thesis is true, or ways how it is being or can be achieved. The idea should always be presented first, with supporting explanation or documentation following. So, a well-structured answer to a question looks like this:

Opener – answer the question

Thesis – Deliver the big picture idea

Supporting point #1 – reason why the thesis is true or way how it will be achieved

Explanation or expansion of point one

Supporting point #2 – reason why the thesis is true or way how it will be achieved

Explanation or expansion of point two

Example:
Question – "Why do the margins in your specialty products division keep declining quarter after quarter?"

Answer – "You're right that we've seen declining margins in this division for the past three quarters. This reflects a corporate decision to invest in the long-term success of the division.

The declining margins you've referred to have been caused by two significant investments in its future success.

The first investment we've made has been in the development of new market segments. We believe this division offers products that differentiate us in the marketplace. In order for the division to realize its full potential, we need to create new markets for the products. To this end, we have invested in xxx marketing initiative.

The second investment has been in the repatriation of some of our production facilities. While this has squeezed the margins in the short-term, we believe the flexibility, supply security and quality control this move allows us will ensure the long-term viability of this important part of the business."

So much about answering questions is about establishing trust and credibility. People are smart. We can tell when someone is avoiding answering, or providing a canned response, or worse, spin. The minute we smell avoidance, we mistrust the speaker and interpret the answer negatively. We need to approach questions and challenges as opportunities, and then answer them directly and honestly. If we are well-prepared and answer in a well-structured, thoughtful manner, Q&As can be powerful leadership opportunities.

CHAPTER SEVENTEEN
LISTEN

When I was a young actor, I had the opportunity to work with a veteran actor who I looked up to. One day after rehearsal he said, "The best actors are really the best listeners." I probably nodded sagely, but I was actually thinking, "What are you talking about? Listening is when I'm not acting. I'm just waiting for my big moment when I get to say my lines." After all, it's called *acting*, not *listening*. I was young, and dumb, and full of myself. It wasn't until years later that I began to understand what he meant. When we really listen, we have no choice but to be fully present. There's no room for the competing voice in my head, I'm not just waiting for my next line, I'm wholly connected and engaged. True listening is hard. It takes more energy and focus than talking. And as a result, truly good listeners are a rare find.

Several years ago, pre-Covid, I was conducting an in-person seminar for around 80 or 90 people. In the middle of my talk, I decided to ask them a simple question: "How many of you can think of someone in your professional lives, past or present, who you would characterize as being an excellent listener?"

I was surprised to see that less than half the room put up their hands. I've repeated this question for many groups I've worked with since and the results are similar: half the people in the room squinch up their faces and stare at the ceiling as they try to think of someone with excellent listening skills; the other half immediately stick their hands in the air. When I probe a little deeper and ask the people who put up their hands if they respected the people that came to mind, if these people were mentors to them, or helped their careers along, the answer is always an emphatic 'yes'. We value good listeners.

I then ask them how they know the person is listening. The answers tend to be along the lines of: they make eye contact, they give visual or verbal feedback (nodding head, 'okay, yeah'), they ask questions when they don't understand, they're not looking at their phone, they don't interrupt, and they are able to offer insight that shows they understood what you were saying. Well, that doesn't sound too hard, does it?! Don't look at your phone, nod, make eye contact and paraphrase back to the speaker what you heard. And if you attend an Active Listening Skills course, this is exactly what they will teach you to do. I've always been somewhat hesitant around teaching listening skills, as it has long been my belief that there is nothing quite so annoying as someone who has recently attended an Active Listening Skills course. They will maintain open body language, nod sympathetically, then lean in while maintaining eye contact and say, "So, if I'm hearing you correctly, you feel that..." It's hard not to feel like they're just going through the motions. You can do everything right and still be a crappy listener.

My next question then, is "Why is listening so hard? What are the barriers to being a good listener?" And here's where things get interesting. This list includes things like: I'm already forming my response in my head while they are talking; I am thinking about the meeting I just came from; I have a hard stop in five minutes and the person doesn't seem to be slowing down and I have to go to the bathroom; the person is boring and I don't really care about what they're talking about; listening is hard, it takes energy! What becomes clear in these responses is that the main barrier to listening is ourselves. Put another way, the voice in our heads prevents us from being fully present which prevents us from truly listening.

The key to being a good listener is in being fully present. Speaking and listening are two sides of the same coin when it comes to being wholly present, so many of my suggestions for being a good listener are similar to those for having presence, because they are about managing the voice in our heads. To be a good listener, we need to quell that voice while the other person is speaking. At the same time, we need to be able to think in silence in order to process what the person is telling us. Here are a few suggestions that will help:

- **Keep notes**
- **Listen structurally**
- **Make eye contact**
- **Pause**
- **Ask questions**

Keep notes

Many of my clients take copious notes during meetings, calls and conversations. But I've noticed something about note-keepers: they rarely check their notes after the fact. The reason that they take notes is that it helps them focus while they listen and, as a result, retain more. Although, apparently, the memory benefit of note taking applies more to handwritten notes than typed. The process of writing notes while we listen forces us to synthesize what we are hearing and translate it into our own words. Note taking works best if you are able to create separation between listening and writing, as opposed to always writing while someone is speaking: this will allow you to think about what you are writing as opposed to capturing verbatim what the person is saying.

Listen structurally

I often jokingly say that my job is to listen to people talk about stuff I don't understand and then repeat it back to them better than they can say it themselves. My clients are experts in their fields and have a depth of knowledge I will never have. As a result, I've trained myself to listen structurally. While my clients talk, I feverishly take notes and while I do, I separate out information from ideas. They will often use acronyms I'm not familiar with (ARPU?, CAGR?, REVPAR?), mixed in with data and explanations of complex issues, all of which I dutifully take note of. But as they are speaking, I will hear linguistic markers, like, "So...", or "Another issue..." or "Because..." These are all indicators that an idea is about to follow. When someone says, "So...", it usually means that their main idea is about to come. If they use the word "Another", it's an indication that they are following some sort of internal mental structure and that a main point is about to follow. When I hear an idea, I will put a box around it in my notes. Then when the client has finished speaking, I can look through my notes with boxes around them and say, "So, really your main issue is this, because of the following three reasons and these are the two ways you can address the issue." It's invariably right. And the client is always happy, because I haven't changed their words, I have just pulled out their main ideas and presented them back to the client in a clear structure. Many people get sucked into the minutiae of what the person is saying. I have the advantage of not under-standing the minutiae which frees me to listen for the structure of the ideas being presented.

Listening structurally is a great way of staying engaged, while providing clarity to a situation. It's a fantastic tool for people leaders, a way of providing clarity without being overly directive. Not only will it give you, the listener, a deeper grasp of what the speaker is saying, it will make them truly feel heard, which is half the goal.

Make eye contact

We generally know that eye contact is a good thing, particu-larly while listening (windows of the soul and all that), but I'm not sure most people fully appreciate why this is the case. As it relates to listening, eye contact is important for two reasons: first, it establishes a genuine connection with the other human being; second, it quietens the voice in our heads. Both are important for listening.

There really is no faking the connection that is established with real eye contact. Not only will you be more attuned to the nuances of what the person is communicating, they will also feel more heard. Good listening isn't just about accurately capturing what is being said, it is about making the speaker feel that the full complexity of what they are trying to communicate has been received. Eye contact helps do this.

The second piece of eye contact is that it helps shut out the voice in our heads. It is very difficult to have a second, parallel soundtrack going in our heads while maintaining eye contact. The voice in our heads is the main barrier to good listening. Often, we are just waiting for the other person to finish speaking so that we can speak the thought we have been formulating while they were talking. This is an extremely frustrating pattern of behaviour for the speaker. Maintaining eye contact will lessen the likelihood of this happening.

Pause

I talk a lot about the importance of pausing while speaking. It is just as important while listening. You may have noticed that the previous points – take notes and make eye contact – are very hard to do at the same time. Give yourself a moment to jot down your notes in silence, or even to think. Pausing allows us to contemplate in silence, which allows us to be more present both when speaking and when listening. Becoming comfortable with pauses is one of the most important things you can do to improve your ability to be present.

Ask questions

There is an art to asking questions. People love being asked questions, but few of us do it well. Asking questions is something I am not naturally skilled at and have had to work very hard at over the years. My instinct is often to listen to what someone says, and then relay a thought or experience that I have had that connects to what they were saying. In my mind, I am trying to create a bridge to what the person is saying by sharing a similar experience of my own, but this can often be interpreted as always bringing it back to myself. This is not an uncommon trait. A number of years ago, I was listening to two participants in a course talking during a break. One of them mentioned that his daughter was leaving the next day for Italy to go on an exchange. The other participant mentioned that his daughter had gone on an exchange the previous year and had loved the experience. I know the second person was trying to find a mutual point of contact, but what actually happened is that it shut down the person whose daughter was leaving for Italy the next day. The conversation turned to the second person talking about *his* daughter's experience. A question is a much more effective way of engaging someone in conversation. It signals that you are interested in them rather than yourself and achieves the same goal as the relayed thought would have. You've probably heard that we have two ears and one mouth for a reason.

Another reason for not asking questions is that people often pretend to understand things they don't. They will nod their heads during a conversation despite not being entirely sure what the other person means. If someone uses an unfamiliar acronym on a call, very few people will interject to ask the meaning of the acronym. I remember once while teaching a course talking about the problem with acronyms a woman in the front row started laughing so hard, she was shaking. I stopped and asked her why she was laughing. She said, "Last week, Tom (her manager), was using an acronym, for like an hour and I had no idea what he was talking about." She turned to her colleague and slapped her on the arm and said, "Then I asked you, and you had no idea, either!" Did either of them stop to ask the meaning of the acronym? Tom had no idea that despite the fact he was talking, no one really understood what he was saying.

Or here's a scenario I have observed that occurs with shocking regularity: a leader walks into a team meeting, talks for awhile, gives some directives, everyone at the table nods agreement and as soon as the leader leaves the room, the team members turn to each other and ask, "So what are we supposed to do?" Why did no one ask questions, despite not truly understanding? Learn to ask questions, even dumb ones (yes, there are dumb questions). You may even want to prepare a few questions prior to a conversation or a meeting. When we ask questions, we not only benefit ourselves, but often the speaker as well.

The thing about listening is that, above all else, it is a choice. Being a good listener requires being fully present and is the opposite side of the coin as speaking with presence. The difference with speaking, however, is that when speaking you have to be at least somewhat present. You may be tracking ahead in your mind, or get lost in your thoughts, or give in to the inner critical voice, but you at least have to be present enough to form and articulate a coherent stream of words. It's very difficult to be writing in the chat column of a Teams meeting while speaking. With listening, it is possible to just check out, to pretend to listen but be completely elsewhere (I have often had to tell clients on video calls that everyone can see the reflection of their phone in their glasses when they surreptitiously check messages during a meeting.) So yes, the skills we have discussed, taking notes, making eye contact, pausing and asking questions, will all help you be a better listener. But first and foremost, you need to make the choice to be present while others are speaking.

CHAPTER EIGHTEEN

BE PRESENT

Whenever I get a request for executive coaching, one of the top objectives of the client is invariably to develop 'Executive Presence'. My response is always, "Great, that's what I do. What do you mean by executive presence?" And the response is typically along the lines of, "I don't know what it is, but I know it when I see it." It is very difficult to achieve an objective you can't define. Turning to the internet, words like 'gravitas', 'charisma' and the 'It Factor' are often used to describe executive presence. Unfortunately, these terms are just as fuzzy and abstract as the original term and provide very little by way of clarity. Suggestions on how to achieve it are many and mostly wildly inconsistent: be still; speak up; make others feel special; understand how others experience you; reflect on your habits; learn how to operate effectively under stress; be a high performer; don't let your appearance be a distraction. These are quotes. And I would suggest fairly unhelpful ones, at that. The real problem with these definitions and suggestions is that they are cosmetic. People think that they need to add a little 'polish'. True presence is much deeper than polish.

My background is theatre. I was trained as an actor, spent fifteen years on stage and another decade as a director. Theatre is all about presence. When you walk on stage, you need to be able to capture the audience and hold them. If you can't do that, you won't have a career. There are actors that you can't take your eyes off, even when they aren't speaking. They have presence. The reason they have presence is that they are wholly present in the moment. It sounds obvious to say, but 'being present' is the root of the word 'presence'. Actors talk about it all the time. The term actors tend to use is 'being in the now'. This sounds simple, but it's actually incredibly challenging. You have memorized lines and it can be very difficult not to jump ahead and think, "What's my next line?" Your director told you that you need to be a foot further upstage for this scene. The lights are hot, and a bead of sweat is trickling down your temple and you wonder if you can casually wipe it away without anyone in the audience noticing. Someone in the front row is unwrapping a candy incredibly slowly and you are wishing they would just GET IT OVER WITH!! The common thread? The voice in your head. When we are caught up in the swirl of our thoughts, we are not present in the moment at all. We are removed from it. And if we are removed from the present, distracted by our thoughts, we will never be our best selves.

The voice in our heads presents the exact same challenges to presence in our daily lives. When we are in a meeting, we are often thinking about what we are going to say next, or still stressed about the previous meeting, or distracted by our phones, or the chat room in the videoconferencing platform. The key to achieving executive presence is in learning to be wholly present and the key to being wholly present is in learning how to manage the voice in our heads. I am going to walk through five ways you can become more present, and in so doing, have more presence:

- **Be prepared**
- **Pause**
- **Breathe**
- **Make eye contact**
- **Manage your nerves**

These are generally good things to do in any situation, but I am going to specifically describe how they help you achieve presence.

Be prepared

I can't overstate the importance of being prepared. I was recently teaching a group of risk professionals at a financial institution and one of the VPs in the group summed up his daily reality: "My whole day is back-to-back calls and usually something has blown up before my first meeting of the day. I dial in five minutes late because the previous call went over, I spend the first ten minutes of the call trying to get up to speed, then I dive in and respond before heading to the next meeting five minutes late. In between I try to get to the bathroom and respond to whatever urgent e-mails came in while I was in the meeting. I'm in constant reaction mode."

I've discussed how I coach clients to prepare for every situation in previous chapters. This practice is essential if you are going to be truly present. It should be part of who you are as a professional. Before you attend a meeting, ask yourself who is going to be attending and what the main point you need them to walk away with is. Before you dial in to a call, jot down a couple of bullet points for yourself on what you would like to get across during the call. When you are preparing to present, focus on what you want to convince your audience of. Preparing your main thoughts in advance will allow you to be more present in the situation because you won't be forming your thoughts on the fly.

Many years ago, I presented with a sports psychologist who talked about full engagement. This gentleman relayed a story about a study that had been done on the mental activity of golfers over the course of 18 holes. Apparently, most golfers don't do a lot of thinking in between holes. Instead, just prior to making a shot, their mental activity ramps up and remains elevated until the shot is completed. He said that for the top golfers, the opposite was true. In between holes, they do a lot of thinking, about what they learned from the previous shot, about what's coming next. But when they go to take their shot, there is very little mental activity: they simply let their body do what it knows how to do. I'm not a golfer, (in fact I aspire to pass through this life without ever swinging a club), but this example made a lot of sense to me: being present (or in the zone), is predicated on being prepared.

Pause

There are many good reasons to pause, both for you as a speaker and for the audience, who are processing what they are hearing. But the main reason, as it pertains to presence, is that a pause will help connect your brain and your mouth. Very few of us are actually thinking about what we are saying while we say it. We are often tracking ahead in our minds, trying to figure out where we are going with the point. A classic example of this is in how people answer questions. The responder will often start with, "That's an excellent question" and continue to answer the question until the finally figure out what their point is, at which point they stop talking. By immediately starting to talk, the speaker is forcing a separation of mouth and mind – my mouth is speaking in the present, but my brain is trying to figure out where to go with the answer. When we do this, the audience doesn't receive the speaker's full impact, because half of them is a few steps ahead.

By pausing, we are giving ourselves a chance to think in silence, so that when we do speak, we can inhabit what we are saying in the moment. Pauses don't have to be long. If we pause briefly between sentences, we have a chance to collect our thoughts before moving on. A useful analogy is how we learn to write. After a sentence, which is a unit of thought, we place a period, followed by a space (I know, a lot of emotional debate between one space or two spaces, but space, nevertheless). When we learn how to write a paragraph, which is a structural unit of thought, we put a line space, or indent, depending on the writing style. And then finally, we learn how to write chapters, which are followed by page breaks. We are trained to guide our readers through our thinking through the use of space. And if you've ever received a document where the formatting has been blown up and there are no spaces, you know the importance of the spaces. Pauses are space. Very few speakers pause enough. Pauses will not only help you, the speaker, stay present in your thoughts, they will help the audience stay present and connected. Listening requires gaps to think about what the speaker is saying. If a speaker doesn't pause enough, the audience is forced to choose between stopping to think, thereby disengaging from the speaker, or not stopping to think, meaning the full weight of the speaker's words aren't felt.

Pausing requires short sentences. Using short sentences is a powerful and easy-to-follow way of speaking, but not as easy as it sounds. Often, the reason for run-on sentences is that our brains are tracking forward and our mouths are constantly trying to catch up, but never can. Run-on sentences are a product of the separation of brain and mouth. Pausing and short sentences go together like peanut butter and jelly. Or ketchup and fries. Or noodles and sauce. You get the picture.

Breathe

Have you ever had a deer-in-the-headlights moment? One where you forget the name of a colleague who you have worked with for ten years and is standing right beside you? I will guarantee that you were holding your breath. Forgetting a line is one of the worst experiences an actor can have. It happens to all of us at some point in our careers. An inexperienced actor will usually panic and blurt out the first thing that comes to mind, which is usually a line from much later in the play and makes no sense. The more experienced actor will pause, breathe, and usually remember the line without anyone in the audience ever noticing. Or, they will think of something to say that fits the scene and everything will progress as normal. A colleague who teaches conflict resolution has a lovely expression: "Pausing to take a breath is the difference between reacting and responding." When we breathe, we allow our brains to function. Time slows down. We feel present in the moment. This allows us to respond in the best possible way. When we hold our breath, we become tense, and our brains seize up.

Unfortunately, it's usually in important situations where we want to exude presence that we tend to tense up and hold our breath. We take short, shallow breaths in our upper lungs. To be fully present, we need to drop the breath down. Breathing helps ground us. Easier said than done. Maybe some of you do yoga, but most of us don't spend much time thinking about where we are breathing. We're still alive, so it must be working, right?

Here's a very simple exercise you can do every day that will help you learn to breathe in a way that will allow you to be more relaxed and more present. If you are sitting in an office chair, chances are there is some lumbar support, a spot where the chair curves inwards and touches the small of your back. It is much easier to drop your breathing down if you have a touchpoint to focus on. Pay attention to the spot where the chair touches your back. If your chair doesn't have lumbar support, you can use a small pillow. Try to breathe into the touchpoint, so that the small of your back gently pushes against it. Do this a couple of times a day, after lunch, before a stressful meeting. It will help ground you in the present. And you have to breathe anyway, so it doesn't take any time out of your day!

Make eye contact

Try to say "ummm" while making eye contact with someone. It's an extraordinarily unnatural thing to do. It feels weird. A speaker will always break eye contact just before saying 'ummm'. The reason is that the speaker wants to go into their not-yet-formed thoughts and needs to break eye contact to do so. They are verbally committed to speaking, but haven't formed the thought yet, so the vocal bridge pops out. It's very difficult to make eye contact while having a separate soundtrack going on in our heads. In other words, *eye contact shuts the voice in our head up*! Shutting up the voice in our head is a useful skill, since it is this that is preventing us from being wholly present. But we still need time to form our thoughts, which is why the previous discussion of pausing is so important. Pausing in silence to form your thoughts, followed by speaking with eye contact will help you be present and connected to the audience.

Manage your nerves

I get nervous for everything, which does make me wonder what I was thinking when I dedicated my life to speaking in public. For many people, nerves are an unpleasant fact of life. It can affect people's career path, and certainly their quality of life. When I get nervous (which is every time I speak), rather than trying to talk myself out of being nervous (which doesn't work), I focus on practical, tangible things I can do. Many of these things have already been discussed: prepare; pause and breathe; make eye contact to quieten the inner voice.

There's one other thing I do: I choose to speak with energy. One of the worst things you can do if you're nervous is to try to appear calm. You're not calm! You're nervous! When we try to appear calm, what we really do is clamp down on our energy, which usually is done be trying to control our breathing and often involves clenching our jaws. We tighten up, which usually forces us into short shallow breathing. We stop pausing. Good speaking requires energy. We need to grab the audience and make them understand why they should care about what we're saying. Nervousness is energy. When we choose to speak with energy, we release the nervous energy in a way that serves the goal of connecting our ideas with the audience. It's like a pressure valve for us and brings our ideas to life for the audience.

In my experience, nerves may diminish with time and experience, but they don't go away. And I find when I'm not a little nervous, I don't have my A game. Choose to speak with energy and focus on being present and the nerves can be a boon rather than a hindrance.

Executive presence is a product of being present. Being present means not being trapped in our heads but connected to the moment. This is true both when speaking and when listening. But being present is not easy. Ask any parent who is trying to respond to a quick email, while making dinner, while their child tries to tell them about their day at school (okay, so that just happened while I was working on this chapter). When we are present, grounded, and connected, we are at our best. I am a practical guy, and I look for practical solutions to challenges. When we prepare, pause, breathe and connect with eye contact, we are physically manifesting presence by being present.

I grew up in the Canadian Prairies, which meant eight months of winter and very little to do other than play and watch hockey. I always loved goalies. Goalies face a lot of pressure and have a reputation for being somewhat odd. Over the years, I've wondered why some nights they seem to be 'on their game' and some nights they can't stop a beachball. There is one goalie in the NHL that I love to watch. Before the game he can be seen in the stands, doing eye exercises, running through in his mind all the things that he is going to face in the upcoming game. In the game, he always seems to be calm and focused. And when he lets in a bad goal, he takes the water bottle from the back of the net, squirts it in the air and focuses on a single drop of water as it falls to the ice. What he is doing is refocusing so that he doesn't get caught up in the voice in his head which is criticizing him for letting in the bad goal. We're all going to let in the odd bad goal. All we can do is ensure we are prepared, focus on the moment, and try to make the next save.

CHAPTER NINETEEN
DON'T BE AN ASSHOLE

Possibly the biggest argument for not being an asshole is that if you are one, I advocated in an earlier chapter for you to be fired. The problem is that nobody thinks they're an asshole. I've coached an awful lot of people over the years, and not one has ever told me that they are an asshole, or a toxic manager, or territorial, or engaging in politics or a bad leader. And yet, they are most assuredly out there. In fact, I suspect that is precisely the reason some of my clients have been sent to me, to improve their 'communication and leadership skills'. Maybe it's you. How can we tell? And more importantly, how can we avoid inadvertently being one? Because, at heart, I believe most of us don't intend to be assholes. It just happens sometimes. It's the other guy.

While no one has ever confessed to me that they are in fact assholes, there are certain patterns of behaviour that people admit to that serve as indicators: "**I can be impatient**"; "**I can be too blunt**"; "**I need a better poker face**"; or the opposite "**I can be hard to read**"; and finally, clients who consistently see the behaviour of others negatively

("**It's not me, it's them**") and are in a constant state of outrage or aggrievement. I'm going to break each of these indicators down and then offer some suggestions on how to address them.

I can be impatient

Well, that's probably because you are focused on the solution and figured out the answer to the problem before the other person was finished talking. Or at least you think you did. And some part of you knows that to be a better leader, you need to let people finish, or figure out the solutions to problems themselves. But on the other hand, they're wasting your time and you have a million other things to do. And it's four o'clock and you've been on calls all day.

The problem with this? Well, you might not be right, because you probably stopped listening halfway through what they were saying. And you just shut down any chance of collaboration. And your impatience/irritability will establish a pattern of people walking on eggshells whenever they're around you. There's no point in having an open-door policy if people are scared to walk through it.

I can be too blunt

I usually hear this from people who are very experienced and quite cynical. You're good at what you do and yet you have seen people less qualified than yourself being promoted. You are resistant to sugar-coating the truth: it's not your fault if people don't want to hear it (special shout out to all the engineers out there). In fact, you may have a fierce pride in your unwillingness to 'play the game'. These are some of my favorite clients to work with because there is an ethical commitment to truth in these individuals.

The problem with this? You can speak the truth all day long, but if you can't get the people around you to accept it, then you're not really contributing anything useful. Plus, you'll then be the person that says, "I told you so." And you were probably right. But nobody likes that person, and you will find yourself increasingly alienated by those around you, aside from a few people who think the same way you do.

I need a better poker face

No, you don't. You need to stop thinking the thought that made you make the expression in the first place. I usually hear this from people who are quick to judge the person who is speaking or the substance of what they are saying. "I have a hard time hiding my feelings when people are saying stuff that is obviously stupid." "This is a waste of time." The more useful and relevant skill is finding the nugget in what the other person is saying instead of dismissing them outright. Or adopting an attitude of curiosity. Why is that person saying or doing what they're saying or doing? How can you help improve things?

I can be hard to read

This is usually a product of clenching your jaw. When your jaw is immobilized, it freezes the highly expressive muscles around your eyes. People like this are often told that once people get to know you that you're great to work with, but that you can come across as aloof or dismissive when they first meet you. The problem with this is that when we don't get any visual feedback from the person we are talking to, we assume the worst, we begin to doubt ourselves, and we see the person as cold or hostile. This may not technically qualify as *being* an asshole, but if you come across as one, it's almost the same thing. Being impossible to read puts the onus on others to push through the first impression (or five).

It's not me, it's them

It's you. Or maybe it's both of you. But you're definitely involved. Just because someone sends you a snarky e-mail doesn't mean you have to respond in kind. Or if you think someone in the organization is being territorial and engaging in 'empire-building', it doesn't mean you have to retaliate. It's easy to be nice to people when they're nice to you. It's easy to be great to work with as long as you get what you want. But the real test of character is how you choose to behave when people aren't nice, and you don't get what you want.

I was working with a client who described getting an aggressive, hostile email from an engineer he had never met. His first response was to pound out an aggressive response. But he was working with me, and thought, "Simon probably wouldn't approve of this." So, he went and made a cup of tea and then wrote a thoughtful, polite response. He said he immediately received an almost overly friendly response. "I think he was embarrassed by his original email when I didn't adopt the same tone." I asked him how long he thought it would have taken to resolve the issue if he had sent his original email. He laughed, and said, "We'd probably still be at it!" When we engage in conflict, whether we initiate it or not, it wastes a lot of time and energy.

I'm sure the indicators above are just scratching the surface. But if you recognize yourself in any of them, here are some practical suggestions on how avoid off-putting communication patterns:

- **Assume the other person has good intentions**
- **Put yourself in your audience' shoes**
- **Listen**
- **Ask meaningful questions**
- **Use positive, inclusive language**
- **Be consistent**

Assume the other person has good intentions
This is quite possible the biggest thing we can do to avoid being an inadvertent asshole. We will often ascribe incredibly negative motivations to the words and actions of others. I often hear it being applied to entire groups: "Oh, that's just marketing throwing it over the wall as usual." When we ascribe negative motivations to others, we listen to everything they say through a filter. It is impossible to build good relationships when this is the case. And you might actually be wrong. Even when the other person is being a jerk, try consciously telling yourself that we all want a good, positive outcome – it might just become a self-fulfilling prophecy.

Put yourself in your audience' shoes
Assholes typically lack empathy. Remember Scrooge? Dude had no empathy. Once he gained empathy, he stopped being such an asshole. Empathy starts with putting yourself in your audience' shoes. What would you be thinking or feeling if you were them? What does the world look like from where they're

sitting? And always remember, we don't know what the other individual is going through. One of the unexpected positive outcomes I noticed during the pandemic was an increase in empathy. Prior to the pandemic, if you asked someone how they were, the answer would invariably be, "Good. Busy." We rarely got to see behind the professional veil people put up. During the pandemic, the answers to, "How are you?" become much more complex and much more honest.

Listen

I wrote a whole chapter about listening, so I won't go rehash it all. But a lot of our poor behaviour comes from us judging the people around us, usually quite harshly. When we judge, we listen through a filter; we are critiquing, countering, commenting on what people are saying while they say it. When we truly listen to what people are saying, we shut the voice in our heads up. The key to this is to maintain real eye contact with the person. This will silence the critical, judging voice in your head long enough to truly hear what the other person is saying, which creates all sorts of opportunities. Real eye contact also establishes a human connection, which will help with our facial expression, our tone of voice and even the substance of what we are saying.

Ask meaningful questions

Asking meaningful questions requires us to try to truly understand what a person is saying. We often get into trouble when we jump to conclusions. It also shows the person that we are actually interested in what they are saying, which means they will be more likely to share meaningful insights. Asking questions is an art and one that many of us lack. The key with asking questions is that you don't always get to the good stuff after the first question – it will often take a follow-up question or two to generate a truly meaningful exchange.

Use positive, inclusive personal language

This one is for the blunt people out there. When you ask a question that starts with, "Well, did you...?" anything that comes after is going to sound like an accusation (as opposed to a meaningful question, as described above). I encourage you to be as direct and clear as possible. I never advocate for sugar-coating or putting spin on something. But by simply tweaking your language so that you are using language that doesn't offend, you can achieve the results you're looking for. Instead of, "Well, did you...", try "One of the things I've often found..." Instead of "The problem is you didn't...", try "What I think we need to do next time is...". The same content can follow, but you won't be pissing people off. Oh, and never get into an email fight ever again.

Be consistent

Being consistent is one of the most important things we can do as leaders. It's not okay to be nice most of the time, but then impatient and angry at others. Be nice all the time. Consistency is the hallmark of professionalism. People around you should know what to expect, otherwise they will start to manage you. The best leaders are clear, direct, kind and consistent. That's the standard you should expect of yourself.

There certainly are assholes in this world. I'm not naïve. Those people should be fired or made to be individual contributors. But many people simply aren't aware that they're assholes. I like to make the comparison to drivers stuck in traffic. Like when you're stuck in traffic and the person next to you won't let you into their lane, even though the two lanes are merging one at a time and it was your turn. What is that person thinking as they stare straight ahead and try to avoid making eye contact? Do they feel bad? Do they justify their behaviour by thinking about someone else's bad behaviour? Do they get home any faster because they didn't let me in? Does it matter? The suggestions I make above are just the principles of good communication. The real work is making the choice to do the right thing. Next time you're stuck in traffic, let the person beside you in; it won't slow you down, and it will make you feel better. And maybe that person let's someone else in down the road and we pay it forward. Same goes for communication.

CONCLUSION

Communication affects everything we do all day long. It is the glue that binds all the various activities of an organization. There's a lot of bad communication out there, both at an organizational and an individual level. You could randomly open this book to a page and do one of the things suggested and it would help improve things. But the real argument I'm making here is for companies and individuals to wholly embrace communication as the most important asset available. To make what is a largely invisible asset visible.

The benefits are endless: increased productivity; increased engagement; better collaboration and innovation. All those buzzwords companies are constantly pursuing. Really, though, better communication results in happier, more productive people.

The thing is, committing to good communication is free. There's no infrastructure investment, no CaaS (Communication as a Service, I just made that up!) required. It is simple, common sense. But it does require effort. That effort needs to be across the entire organization: top down, bottom up; flattened hierarchy. Everywhere.

I truly believe that both companies and individuals that commit to building a better communication culture will thrive. It's all there for the taking – it just needs to be made a priority.

www.ingramcontent.com/pod-product-compliance
Lightning Source LLC
Chambersburg PA
CBHW030940180526
45163CB00002B/643